REBUILDING
LONDON

REBUILDING LONDON

IRISH MIGRANTS IN POST-WAR BRITAIN

MIKI GARCIA

First published 2015
Reprinted 2022

The History Press
97 St George's Place,
Cheltenham, Gloucestershire, GL50 3QB
www.thehistorypress.co.uk

British Library Cataloguing in Publication Data.
A catalogue record for this book is available from the British Library.

ISBN 978 1 84588 877 0

Typesetting and origination by The History Press
Printed by TJ Books Limited, Padstow, Cornwall

Trees for LYfe

CONTENTS

ACKNOWLEDGEMENTS

Thank you so much to all of the people who answered my questions and inspired me along the way: Peter O'Driscoll, John Jones, James O'Sullivan, Doris Daly, Jim Duggan, Tony Donovan, Maureen Fitzgerald, Michael Doyle, Séamus O'Cionnfhaola, Pat Griffin, John Hurley, Robert Sheehy, Brendan O'Sloan, Steve Martin, William Thompson, Bernard Canavan and Áine Ní Lanagáin.

I would like to thank to all the librarians and workers at the various libraries, archives and research centres for helping me to find documents and photos. I am also grateful to the Irish Embassy in London.

I am also deeply indebted to my editor, Beth Amphlett, for professionally dealing with my persistent demands and helping to make this book happen.

And finally, thank you to all the people who allowed me to share their stories at Arlington House and on the streets of London, as well as at various Irish centres over a cup of tea.

All images are provided courtesy of Brent Council, Brent Archives.

INTRODUCTION

This book considers the role of Irish migrants and, in particular, how they worked and lived – primarily in London – during the peak years for immigration after the Second World War.

The war took away the majority of capable young men – more than 3.5 million served in the British Army. To replace their workforce, women and immigrants took the jobs formerly performed by men. After all, Britain needed to keep the country going before, during and after the war, and to rebuild the bombed and destroyed infrastructure.

The Irish had been the most substantial minority group within the British population from the eighteenth century onwards. For approximately 100 years before the Great Famine in the mid-1850s, the Irish had been a strong and stable workforce in Britain who came in droves to harvest, heave coal and work in all kinds of industries to develop the country. The Great Famine was a decisive historical event as it pushed more than a million Irish people out of Ireland – chiefly to North America, but also to Britain and other countries. The impact of the Irish immigrants was especially significant in politics, in the labour market, trade unions and the Roman Catholic Church on both sides of the Atlantic.

A steady stream of Irish immigrants had been flooding into the US but the direction of the mass migration eventually turned back to Britain due to the aftermath of the Great Depression in the 1930s, as well as the strict immigration laws introduced by the American Government.

The establishment of the Irish Free State in 1921 had failed to pave the way for economic growth. For most people, emigration was vital for survival rather than an opportunity for a better future. The fact that the State was neutral during the Second World War made ordinary people's lives even harder. After the war ended, the Republic of Ireland's economy remained dormant, even though other western European countries were enjoying the post-war reconstruction economic boom. The Irish economy simply could not cope with the strains of independence, despite the fact that the country received a substantial amount of post-war aid. During the 1950s, the gross national product, or GNP, continued to decline each year and Ireland officially had the most sluggish economy in Western Europe, typically dubbed as 'a capitalist country without capital'. In Ireland, times were hard, with no job prospects, bleak rural life, unfair marriage practices and an inflexible Roman Catholic Church, amongst other things.

It is unsurprising, therefore, that Irish emigration in the 1950s was at its highest since the Great Famine. Attracted to the post-war reconstruction boom between 1951 and 1961, more than 400,000 people – or one-sixth of the population – crossed the pond. Within this group, two-thirds of Irish immigrants ended up in London. According to the British Census of 1951, one-third of the people born in the twenty-six counties were living in Greater London. Because the majority of the post-war immigrants from Ireland were Catholic, rural and from the South, the term 'Ireland' in this book generally is used for Republic of Ireland, and 'the Irish' are the people from the Republic.

Going to British cities was more like a rural-urban internal migration, just like Scottish or Welsh people moving to larger English cities; it was a completely different situation from the transatlantic or long-haul international migration. Irish emigration to Britain has often been done as a result of rather impetuous decisions, and the principal reason has always been economic. A lack of major industries in Ireland resulted in very little opportunity for steady employment. Britain, meanwhile, offered jobs that were not available in Ireland. Close geographical proximity and historical connections made London and other British cities popular as major centres of Irish settlements.

During the post-war years, scores of newcomers who were arriving in British cities on a daily basis had to fit in as quickly as they could amid changing political, economic and social climates. Compared to other immigrants from Commonwealth countries, Irish people's cultural and characteristic similarities to the British ensured that Irish people remained in 'a curious middle place' within the British system. Their de facto British status and invisibility within British society made their lives slightly complicated, as they were called 'citizens of the Irish middle nation'.[1]

To cater for Irish immigrants' specific needs, social clubs, county associations, dancehalls, newspapers, GAA clubs, religious and non-religious charities and Irish businesses quickly sprang up, forming a thriving Irish community. Priests and nuns also played a significant part in Irish immigrants' lives. As British rule had influenced Ireland for such a long time, Irish people know what it meant to be treated unfairly. To fight against injustice, albeit in a different context, Irish trade unionists had indispensable roles in all industries.

The two most conspicuous Irish occupations during the post-war reconstruction period were nurses – who were the backbone of NHS hospitals from its inception – and navvies, who were involved in building all essential infrastructures. Quite a few construction workers who came to England with little or no money in their pockets eventually became wealthy and successful businessmen, simply by seizing the moment. Some of the most prominent people who have become synonymous with large company names are John Murphy from County Kerry, Pat McNicholas from County Mayo, Michael Clancy from County Clare, Pat Fitzpatrick from County Cork, Michael Joseph

Gleeson and Peteen Lowery both from County Galway, to name but a few. Needless to say, these bosses were always partial towards hiring their own countrymen, who were incessantly arriving.

It is not an exaggeration to say that without their hard work and sweat, Britain would never have been rebuilt after the war. As Donall MacAmhlaigh, the author of *An Irish Navvy: The Diary of an Exile*, put it: 'Here in Dublin, there are Irish of all kinds – rich, poor, intelligent and ignorant – but in England, for the most part, there is only one kind of Irishman and that is the worker.'

This was especially true during the post-war period.

1

IRELAND

It is a good country to die in.
You can always get a good funeral in Ireland.
But it is not a good country to live in.
It is a country of enormous funerals.
Priests, policemen, publicans and politicians.

John Broderick[2]

You cannot talk about Ireland without addressing its history of emigration. Some of the distinguished characters of the history of Ireland can be explained through British colonisation, oppression and, as a consequence, poverty and emigration. Most famously, Ireland is known for the Great Famine, a key point in the history of the Irish Diaspora. However, Irish people have been populating all corners of the globe for centuries. The vast majority of Irish migrants were involuntary immigrants, who had to leave in large numbers to survive or earn a living, especially when times were bad. The people who left home believed that there was a better life elsewhere.

The establishment of the Irish Free State in 1922, which consisted of twenty-six counties (officially later renamed Éire), didn't change much for the better. The biggest change was that after the British were gone, Catholic Church authority became clearly visible in all

aspects of Irish life and, arguably, more powerful than the Free State
government.

Ireland was neutral and didn't join the Second World War.
The wartime neutrality cost Ireland and Irish people politically and
economically during the post-war years. Most imports, such as coal
and food, were stopped during the 'Emergency'. In terms of the
North-South political relationship, neutrality reinforced partition
and strengthened unionist rule in Northern Ireland, which became
the serious problem of the post-war isolation of the northern Irish
Catholic community. Consequently, a large inflow of post-war Irish
immigrants contributed to the Irish Republican Army activities in
Britain in the subsequent years of the Troubles.

Referring to a mass exodus from Ireland, the post-war period was
famously described as 'the decade of the vanishing Irish who disappeared in silence'.[3] During this decade, one of the most popular Irish
songs was called 'The Boys of Barr na Stáide', written by Irish poet
Sigerson Clifford. It is about his childhood friends in Cahirciveen,
Kerry, who fought the Black and Tans, and had a good time with him
but are now all scattered: 'And now they toil on foreign soil, where
they have gone their way, deep in the heart of London town or over
in Broadway.'

MAKING A LIVING

People migrate for all sorts of different reasons, be they economic,
political or social. Their motives and migration routes also vary,
depending on their education, gender, age and family background.
The general 'push factors' that drove Irish people out of the country
during the post-war period was mainly economic, due to the lack
of steady employment opportunities, particularly in rural areas. But
the situation was a vicious circle: underdeveloped areas in Ireland
remained the same due to a lack of a workforce as capable people
who should have been productive had left in search of work.

The most common reason for Irish citizens to leave their homeland
has been always to earn a living. An Anti-Partition League report of
1957 surmised that Irish people lacked national sentiment, particularly in the younger generations. The report shows that the primary
concern for the vast bulk of the Irish-born population was to make
a living and, if possible, 'put some money aside'.

When the Irish Free State was established in 1921, everybody
expected that the state would soon become industrialised and trans-
form the whole region. Sadly Ireland was unable to recover from the
slump and continued to suffer from the debts incurred in the civil war.
William T. Cosgrave from the Cumann na nGaedheal government
was more focused on improving the agricultural sector rather than
industrialisation. As a result, de-industrialisation became a common
sight in most parts of Ireland, which remained part of the British
market. As a matter of fact, the majority of Irish industries in Ireland
were either owned or controlled by the British.

Instead of attempting to improve the situation with new economic
policies, the Irish people concentrated on restoring Irish culture such
as Gaelic language, music and sport and the rigid values of the Catholic
Church. This meant that even creative people, such as writers and artists,
joined the migration trend due to the rigid censorship establishment
after the Censorship of Publications Act came into force in 1929. In 1950,
poet Robert Graves famously described this as 'the fiercest literary censorship this side of the Iron Curtain'. Cork writer Frank O'Connor
was also critical of the government: he saw it as attempting to destroy
the character and prospects of Irish writers in their own country. John
Broderick, a writer from Athlone who migrated to England, described
Ireland as 'very self-destructive'. His book *The Pilgrimage* was among
countless books that were banned in Ireland. Whether one likes it or not,
however, taking a boat was a sensible thing to do. Patrick Kavanagh wrote
in his autobiographical novel *The Green Fool*:

> I decided to go to London. Ireland was a fine place to daydream in, but
> London was a great materialist city where my dreams might crystallize

into something more enduring than a winning smile on the face of an
Irish colleen – or landscape.[4]

Because so many people left between 1841 and 1961, the population of Ireland was almost halved. Late marriage and low marriage
rates also contributed to the population loss throughout post-war
period. The standard of living was getting worse rather than better.
The Republic's total labour force in the 1950s was almost the same as
at the foundation of the state.

The post-war period of reconstruction was a time of great progress
in some European countries. While these countries began to enjoy a
better standard of living, the Republic of Ireland – which came into
force and was renamed in 1949 – was stagnant in many ways and
suffered from chronic unemployment and emigration throughout the
decade. Ireland was the only country in Europe in which the con-
sumption of goods and services fell, and frequent strikes, such as the
Dublin Unemployed Association marches in 1953, only highlighted
the severity of the problem. Although the Irish Republic became
independent and received a substantial number of grants and loans by
1950, Irish unemployment still depended very much on conditions
in Britain and Ireland was thus unable to become self-sufficient or
build its own industries.

The agricultural sector was not performing well, either. The drudg-
ery of rural life resulting from the lack of power, water and sanitation
only encouraged farmers to leave. During the post-war years, many
small farmers gave up agriculture as they could not afford new
technologies to compete with bigger farmers with land and so were
not able to support their families. As few employment opportunities were available in rural areas in Ireland, they were left with no
choice but to go elsewhere. Consequently, the country lost a large
amount of farmers. Between 1950 and 1959, three government
departments – Agriculture, Local Government and Lands (a scheme
restricted in the *Gaeltacht*, or Irish-speaking region) – provided grants
for the installation of water in rural homes, but by 1959, only 1,600

households had benefitted from these schemes (as many of them had gone by this time). Subsequently, by 1961, agriculture had declined by nearly 50 per cent, to a level not seen since 1926 and the agricultural industry lost its position as the leading employment sector.

The Irish Government did not completely ignore the issue of population decline, although it was not really keen on preventing its citizens leaving the country. In 1948 it set up the Commission on Emigration and Other Population Problems, acknowledging for the first time that emigration was an integral feature of Irish economy and needed to be considered in the policy-making process. After seven years, the commission finally issued *The Report* in 1955, which analysed the current situation such as the impact and patterns of emigration and its consequences. The government did not encourage emigration, but *The Report* did not offer any concrete solutions or remedies to stop it: because 'going away' was the country's real solution. *The Leader* magazine reported that many politicians were privately more relieved than disturbed by the post-war emigration, because 'if emigration were to be stopped tomorrow conditions favourable to social revolution might easily arise'.

In a mediocre and rather vague attempt, however, the government did ask its people who had already left to come back. On 2 January 1950, the *Cork Examiner* printed an article entitled 'Not enough skilled labour for building programme "Return", says Taoiseach, or Prime Minister, to emigrants':

Speaking on the government's housing programme in a talk broadcast from Radio Éireann last night, An Taoiseach (J.A. Costello) said that during the Second World War, many of Ireland's skilled workers had emigrated. It was now desirable, as well in the nation's interest, that they return home. They would find work in Ireland at payment rates at least as good as, if not better than, what they earned abroad, and they would have an assurance that for the foreseeable future, they would have constant work in the building industry. There were over 100,000 homes to be built, said An Taoiseach, and by the time that number was completed, a great many more houses would require reconstruction. We had not enough of skilled men and we needed these urgently if we were to get on with the job…the new state inherited a really formidable and terrible burden of slums hovels and insanity dwellings. Years of neglect and over crowding in cities and towns during the nineteenth century produced shamefully bad housing conditions, particularly in Dublin where the slums were a disgrace to any civilised people…the Government recently announced their decision to undertake a programme costing over the years about £120 millions, which would provide 110,000 new dwelling houses in ten years and within seven years, would adequately equip the country with modern hospitals. That programme was now being put into effect with accelerating speed so as to provide now houses in all parts of the country as well as 33 new hospitals…Christian family life required a decent dwelling for every family…

This evasive and rather controversial article was read by many Irish immigrants in England with interest. The majority of them responded to it with scepticism, annoyance and even anger. One of them, Micheal O'Siochain, wrote a letter to the editor:

It is quite obvious that it applied only to skilled building workers … it doesn't seem to be a call that is received here with the enthusiasm that a national call of its apparent urgency is entitled to.

Despite the economic depression in the country as a whole, the capital of the republic was undergoing a transformation. In the 1950s, there were plenty of employment opportunities in Dublin. The Bord Failte, or tourist board, was created in 1952. Trams had been phased out, and so tram tracks were removed from the streets. Buses were typically packed at the weekend for those migrant workers from rural areas to go home. Long-awaited development and slum clearance plans were executed. Scores of cottage houses were built rapidly, along with hundreds of balcony block flats and council buildings.

Dublin Airport expanded rapidly; runways were extended and terminals were enhanced in order to deal with foreign airlines such as British European Airways, Sabena and BKS Air Transport. Subsequently, Ireland's own airline, Aer Lingus, grew swiftly with the help of economist Garret FitzGerald, future Taoiseach. Its first transatlantic flight from Shannon-Dublin to New York was in 1958. Although it was still expensive to fly for the average person, the development of Shannon Airport brought a large number of Americans to Ireland. Used as a refuelling stop, Shannon Airport was the entry point into Europe. American presidents, politicians, film stars and high-profile business people stopped over and, as a result, the first duty-free shop was opened here. This is also the place where Irish coffee was invented and served for the first time.

The post-war period was seen as a complex and tumultuous time for the Irish economy until the Secretary of the Department of Finance, Kenneth Whitaker, called for free trade and an end to protectionism. His White Paper, entitled *The First Programme for Economic Expansion* and published in November 1958, became a landmark in Irish economic history and Ireland finally underwent structural reforms in the 1960s.

THE CHURCH

Even though the post-Famine years were long gone, the landlord mentality and logic lingered on in society and made ordinary people's lives intolerable. On top of this, the Church became a dominating figure and represented the ultimate authority in Ireland.

English control, begun in 1171, continued to influence the Irish way of life and helped form national as well as religious identities of Irish people. Since the establishment of the Irish Free State in 1922, the control exerted by the Roman Catholic Church became more conspicuous, particularly in the fields of education, health and welfare services. Catholicism played a critical part in the formation of Irish society and it was overwhelmingly the centre of people's lives, whether one was religious or not.

After the post-Famine period, the Roman Catholic Church in Ireland embarked on major church-building projects in both rural areas and towns. As a result, churches prospered all across Ireland and they often had six Masses on a Sunday to accommodate a vast number of churchgoers who flocked to fulfil their religious obligations.

Because religious practices were rife, it was not unusual that work was frequently interrupted. Jim Duggan from Waterford, who came to London in the 1950s, recalled his workplace in Ireland: 'When the bells of church rang at 12 o'clock each day, we had to kneel down on the job and say the angelus prayer. And there was a prayer meeting during the day, too.'[5]

Local newspapers in Ireland unanimously carried news on the Pope and the Catholic Church catechism and propaganda on a daily basis, as well as all kinds of stories related to Catholicism around the world. Catholicism dominated everyone's life. The Catholic Church soon became so powerful that it was able to enforce censorship in newspapers, books, advertisements and arts, especially in the areas that were considered against Catholic dogma, such as sexuality.

During this period, Church-run institutions such as industrial schools, homes for unmarried mothers, Magdalene laundries and other institutions gained absolute authority. Some of them existed for many decades prior to the 1950s and grew to be authoritarian institutions, regardless of their original intention. In many cases, those children and grown-ups who had to endure abuse there were left in appalling physical and psychological circumstances.

Although the Church did not assume an obvious political role, its influence in government became increasingly conspicuous. One of the examples was the Mother and Child Scheme, which was proposed by the Minister for Health Noel Browne in 1950. The scheme was intended to provide free maternity care for mothers and healthcare for children, but the then Archbishop of Dublin, John Charles McQuaid, among others, feared that the scheme would pave the way for abortion and birth control.

Direct intervention by the Catholic Church in public life like this was not unusual; the Catholic Church typically encouraged traditional women's roles such as wives and mothers, and church authorities were adamant that it was the right of parents to provide the care for their children. This healthcare programme was engulfed in crisis from the beginning, simply because it had provoked the hierarchy. Browne's proposal ended disastrously as he was isolated and did not receive any support from his colleagues at all. The government yielded, as was often the case when the Church and State came into conflict.

During this time, the Irish Department of Health was conscious that Britain was developing the welfare system, but showed only lukewarm interest. Fianna Fáil's Social Welfare Act in 1952 rationalised and finally extended national health insurance, unemployment insurance, and widows' and orphans' schemes. But compared to Britain, which by this time included Northern Ireland, benefits in the Republic were relatively meagre and not for all.

EMIGRATION

Many politicians such as James Dillon, the leader of Fine Gael at that time, were aware that a substantial number of people left not simply due to economic pressure, but also for other reasons; he suggested that these emigrants consisted of 'some of whom had the temerity to be already above the poverty line, to improve their own condition and even that of their children'. *The Report* by the Commission on Emigration also suggested that emigration was rife even where land was relatively good. James Dillon concluded that 'even employed persons are leaving their jobs for more highly paid employment in Britain'.

One of the main social reasons – especially for women – to emigrate was unfair marriage practices. Marriage in Ireland was at one time directly linked to land ownership. But after the Great Famine, rather than the traditional custom of subdividing land between siblings, only one child would inherit the land.

The typical marriage arrangement (which remained in place until the 1950s), especially for medium and large farmers, was the 'match': an arranged marriage for the son nominated to succeed to the family farm. The match reflected parental control, as well as that of the husband-to-be: the woman had to bring a dowry, or 'fortune' as it was called, with her. The money was typically used to support the other children in the household, and often assisted their emigration.

This marriage practice almost made it impossible for women to even find a husband to get married locally. As a result, many women remained single or emigrated, as they could not afford dowries, while male siblings who could not inherit the land also contributed to the high rate of emigration. There is a strong connection between high emigration and low marriage rates, as they were the products of the same root cause.

Furthermore, there were no available jobs for women in the locality, but women in the workforce were not common in Ireland in those days. Emigration seemed to be the only option for women who wanted to work.

There were huge differences between rural and urban areas not only in transport, electricity and water supplies, but social services such as health, welfare, entertainments and recreational centres were non-existent in some regions. Youngsters in rural areas had nowhere to go, so they were naturally attracted to the exciting city life outside their villages. They were all too aware of the better conditions elsewhere as they received letters from migrants, which were often accompanied with remittances, nothing but positive newspaper articles about successful immigrant stories and life in foreign lands. Local Irish newspapers advertised plenty of job opportunities in Britain on a daily basis and the emigrants themselves would regularly return home on holidays looking well-dressed and sophisticated with accounts (possibly exaggerated) that never failed to make a vivid and lasting impression on young people's mind.

The Commission on Emigration acknowledged that – especially for youngsters – rural areas appeared to be 'dull, drab, monotonous, backward and lonely – a view, however, which many would regard as superficial'. In certain rural areas, the only entertainment was to go to see an occasional GAA match.

Another important factor was a herd mentality. A considerable number of Irish people left for British cities by following their friends, relatives, or the other people they know from home. Many people followed the crowd without questioning; it was a natural thing to do. Rural youngsters often wished to escape the monotony of daily routines of rural life and left after hearing from their friends and family members about the fun and exciting city life in London and other British cities. Some people just left home without planning or thinking as a result of making a snap decision, especially after seeing close friends leaving for England, or a fight or an argument with their father.

An Irish immigrant who just gave his name as 'Gerard' recalled that his decision to leave home came fairly quickly and easily:

I came to England in the 1950s, when there was a great demand for Irish labour. One Saturday night I was in Dublin and I went to a dance in O'Connell Street and ran into an old friend of mine whom I'd known in college and we had been in digs together; he'd qualified and come to England. This was on Saturday night, we had a jolly good drink and I went back to the hotel with him and spent the night, went down to the North Wall and I got the boat to England.[6]

Another migrant, 'Tony', decided to come to London after the Second World War, having lost his parents:

My mother died when I was 12. My father was a gamekeeper and had a tied house in Cork. He had a heart attack and died at 51. I was 16 then. I was working as a junior cadet and only realised that I was not going to get an officer's job. I had no responsibilities so I came to London in 1955, when I was 19. I had no one here. I have relatives in Connecticut in the US, so I thought about going there before coming to London. But it is 3,000 miles away, and if I didn't like it, or if

anything went wrong, I cannot come back. But if I come here, I can
always come back to Ireland. I thought it was easier. This country has
been good to me. As an Irish man, I think I did well.[7]

The majority of parents were supportive and encouraged their children
to emigrate. Donall MacAmhlaigh, who worked in various English
cities including London, recounted in his autobiography how he made
his mind up to come to England in the first place, although he was
rather reluctant:

[My] mother saw the ad. in the paper: 'Stokers wanted. Live in. Apply
Matron, Harborough Rd. Hospital, Northampton.'

'You could give it a chance,' she said, 'for surely God put it in your
way …

My mother called in from the street one of the children playing
around there and sent her off to the shop for a sweet cake so that
we'd have a celebration in honour of the occasion. As she took up
the pot to make the tea, I could see that her eyes were brimming
with tears.[8]

Many clergy expressed grave concern over the situation as there were
so many young, innocent teenagers leaving Ireland – some were as
young as 15. Father Ambrose Woods, a parish priest, was involved in
welfare work and helped countless Irish people in his bomb-damaged
parish in Southwark. He later played a major role in the development
of the Irish Centre in Camden. He condemned the parents who
encouraged their children to leave: 'I can only call it the murder of
the Irish innocents. There are fathers and mothers who allow their
immature and uninformed children to go to England.'[9]

Priests believed that these young, naïve and inexperienced emigrants were immediately exposed to temptation and moral danger in
the metropolis. The Director of the Central Statistics Office in 1956
pointed out that three out of every five children born in Southern
Ireland could expect to emigrate.

SOCIAL OUTCASTS

Many studies found that the status of female workers in Ireland was significantly lower than in Britain. Domestic servants, for example, were considered to be 'an inferior form of life by both employers and the community at large', according to the Irish Housewives' Association, or IHA. Hilda Tweedy established the IHA in 1942 in an attempt to gain recognition for the right of housewives, and it became affiliated with the International Alliance of Women in 1947. The IHA also functioned as a pressure group to address the injustices and the needs of Irish women, both domestically and internationally.

The IHA also pointed out that 'the domestic worker in Great Britain gets recognition as a human being while she does not get it here'. Many women were fed up with Ireland because of their low status and harsh conditions of work. In Britain there was better pay, better facilities and better prospects for domestic servants, though

Young Irish women gather around a piano at Marion Women's Hostel, Hornsey Lane Gardens, Highgate.

many typically dreamed of working as teachers, nurses or in the office – more respectable jobs with promotion opportunities.

Fr McSweeney, Director of the Irish Centre in Camden Town, wrote that the 1950s surge of emigrants contained a burgeoning number of what he called 'social casualties', which included alcoholics, unmarried mothers, prostitutes and petty criminals. These people were a grave source of concern to the Church authorities. Irish priests living in London considered major British cities 'dumping ground for the unwanted and the deviant'. There had been a long tradition of pregnant women – both single and married – leaving Ireland to give birth in Britain or fleeing from broken marriages or domestic violence as abortions and divorce were illegal.

During those days, when women fell pregnant out of wedlock in Ireland, very few family members were supportive or able to help raise illegitimate children as their own, and often the majority of them turned their backs on their pregnant relative. Those women who had their babies in Ireland often ended up incarcerated in Catholic institutions such as the Magdalene asylums, where they were forced to work as de facto slaves. The conventional crime the women and girls who went to Magdalene committed was 'bearing children out of wedlock' or 'leaving abusive husbands'. A booklet called *Justice for Magdalenes* stated:

> [The punishment was] often a lifetime of 'penitence' spent in the service of the Sisters of Charity, the Sisters of Mercy, Good Shepherd and other orders, performing domestic chores … harsh, thankless chores such as laundering prison uniforms, clerical washing, hotel linens cleaning and caring for elderly nuns or their ageing peers, still trapped behind the walls of Ireland's numerous convent laundries … They were told to forever hide their shame inside these walls, work under harsh, Spartan conditions; driven unmercifully by the sisters and often abused by them as well.[10]

Vulnerable Irish domestic workers were often seduced or raped, not just in Ireland, but in Britain as well. The overwhelming majority of these girls were typically powerless and therefore had no options when they got pregnant. Becoming pregnant was not only socially and legally unacceptable, but having a baby meant that they would lose their job. As a desperate measure, infanticides frequently occurred all across Ireland throughout the early 1900s, as evidenced by various cases reported by local newspapers. Mothers – often young, poor and Roman Catholic – killed their illegitimate newborns by suffocating, strangling, drowning, poisoning and abandoning them in hidden spots; their sisters or other family members were often actively involved in the murder.[11]

As it was socially unacceptable to have a baby outside of marriage, Irish women typically went to England, preferably without anyone knowing the real reason for their departure. There had been a legal framework for legal adoption in England since the aftermath of the First World War, but Ireland did not provide the same system in the early 1950s. Many Irish women had their babies adopted and returned home as if nothing happened, while the small minority stayed to bring up their babies in England, where they could remain anonymous.

To cater for those women, scores of hostels for unmarried mothers, mother and baby homes and foster houses in London and other British cities existed. The majority of them were run by the Church and Irish nuns, such as the Dames of Saint Joan in Leigham Court Road and Saint Pelagius's in Highgate, which was run by the Sisters of the Sacred Heart. However, hospital almoners acknowledged that frightened girls often refused to go into a mother and baby home run by nuns, as a convent typically had strict rules and regulations in the name of rehabilitation. Under the circumstances, the majority of these mothers preferred non-Catholic or non-denominational homes, an expression considered by Catholic organisations as 'the first step to giving up their faith'. There were also hostels run by lay organisations, such as the Legion of Mary in Bayswater, who helped uncounted young, pregnant and unmarried mothers. The Catholic Truth Society published a pamphlet called *The Unmarried Mother and Her Child*, written by Mary Walsh, and distributed it to young mothers.

Fr Seamus Fullam from Longford recalled:

> Once those girls made their escape and came to London, they'd be put in touch with us and we'd send them on to the Crusade of Rescue. This was an organisation which helped and cared for girls in crisis ... The Crusade helped those girls who had to give their babies up for adoption. Nine out of ten mothers went for adoption because they simply couldn't go home with their babies ... In those days, too, we used to have people from the Legion of Mary to meet the girls off the train at Euston. They were terrified at their predicament, but they couldn't stay at home ... Usually, the girl's mother would be more understanding, but the father was often unchristian. They kicked their daughter out, and that was it ... Some poor girls never went home.[12]

Fr P. Harvey of the Crusade of Rescue noted 'an appalling number' of girls applying to the Crusade for help. But Crusade homes were simply too overcrowded and 'the disgruntled mother' had to apply to the council for help, which resulted in the baby returning to Ireland in due course, with or without its mother. The council worked in order to find the child a Catholic home across the water, in an attempt to ensure that it remained with relatives. While some Catholic organisations such as the Southwark Catholic Rescue Society labelled the council as uncooperative, the reality was that they had been burdened with the job of placing illegitimate children in Ireland at the rate of two or three a week.

A *Catholic Herald* article on 5 March 1954 reported that the caseload of the Roman Catholic social workers was out of all proportion to their number and that it was impossible to look after all the unmarried mothers arriving in London. In 1955 the Crusade of Rescue claimed that it could not cope with the large numbers (estimated to be hundreds annually) while the Child Protection and Rescue

Society of Ireland reported that the situation appeared to be particularly bad in the London area. The number of births were never officially recorded and many babies would be quietly handed over to the adoptive parents, mainly in the US. An estimate suggests more than 2,000 babies were sent there during the 1950s and 1960s.

A plethora of Catholic and non-Catholic organisations, social workers and rescue societies came to the aid of those who needed help and guidance, while the Catholic Women's League in the Brentwood diocese attempted to interest the heads of Catholic grammar schools in fostering a social welfare training among suitable girls.

Many people were critical about Irish babies growing up in non-Catholic foster homes. Mrs H. Halpin, Chairman of the Children's Committee, called for the children to be returned to Ireland, saying that 'with the co-operation of the Eire authorities, the children will now be able to live happy, normal lives in their own families, back home where their unfortunate mothers came from'. This view, unfortunately, simply wasn't realistic.

The Catholic Rescue Society in London also expressed concern over the shortage of Catholic foster homes but with too many cases to handle, it had no option but to rely on non-Catholic foster homes and institutions.

In 1954, the National Council for the Unmarried Mother and Her Child, now known as Gingerbread, published the annual report *The Unmarried Mother and Her Child* for the year 1952-1953. This progressive charity was found in 1918 by Lettice Fisher to reform the Bastardy Acts and Affiliation Order Acts laws and to provide alternative accommodation to the workhouse for mothers and babies.

According to the report, there were comparatively few trained Catholic social workers to help and guide unmarried expectant mothers, which made it impossible to cope with the alarming number of those girls and women. The report suggested that an unmarried mother should raise her child rather than have them adopted or placed in an institution, as 'it can never represent the Catholic ideal of family life'. An increasing number of pregnant girls would have been happy to bring up their babies by themselves but unfortunately, very few girls could actually manage to keep them. The big problem for these young mothers was the lack of lodgings where they could leave their babies in care of the landlady or an affordable nursery while they were at work. These women also needed practical and material assistance to deal with the difficulties, problems and responsibilities of the situation they found themselves in; this support, according to the report, should ideally be provided by trained social workers.

Although the law at that time did not permit consent to adoption to be given until a child reached at least six weeks of age, it was common practice to arrange for an illegitimate child to be placed with foster parents at a much earlier stage and for the legal formalities of adoption to be dealt with once the six-week interval had elapsed. The report fiercely criticised this process, as it deprived the unmarried mother of that 'admittedly very short period in which to consider her position calmly and decide without pressure whether she is in a position to accept the responsibility of bringing up her child on her own'.

The high rate of illegitimacy within the Irish community was clearly visible. Irish girls having babies out of wedlock in England was widely reported in British newspapers. The London County Council's Children's Committee wrote that 'immorality is rife among such immigrants'. Although the vast majority of Irish girls remained faithful to the Catholic Church, the greater freedom, lack of friends and no parental control or supervision were common reasons for some Irish immigrants losing faith.

The Southwark Rescue Society's records show that in 1956 there were 137 Irish girls who had become pregnant in Britain applying for help, while 44 had fallen pregnant in Ireland. These figures were higher than the previous highest, set in 1950. The majority of these decided to have their babies in Britain, because they knew that facilities were better than Ireland during a time when the infant mortality rate was high. The Irish Department of Local Government and Public Health reported that one out of every four illegitimate infants died within the first year of life.

Furthermore, quite a few unmarried Irish women who were already in Britain bore mixed-race babies, which was considered particularly shameful by many in Irish society at the time. Most of the babies were adopted but a small minority of them brought their child up on their own. When they had a black baby they typically kept it secret from their family in Ireland. It was not uncommon that those women went home for Christmas without their babies.

The causes of illegitimacy were a hugely complicated problem and broken homes or ignorance were not the root cause. The report found that the youngest unmarried mothers dealt with by the department were just fourteen years old. Young Irish unmarried pregnant girls continued to come from all walks of life, including university students as well as girls from the sheltered atmosphere of old-fashioned children's homes. Having been enticed to England by employment agencies and started working, they were often left to their own devices.

Unmarried women who got pregnant in Ireland or Britain in those days caused complex problems to themselves and society, as well as their children, who often suffered from mental scars of the insecurity of their early life and frequently experienced subsequent discrimination due to the stigma of illegitimacy. One of the aims of the National Council for the Unmarried Mother and Her Child and other organisations such as the Crusade of Rescue was to reduce the atmosphere of abnormality and insecurity that often surrounded the early life of the illegitimate child.

Social casualties also contained many young teenagers. Jennifer Worth, the author of *Call the Midwife: A True Story of the East End in the 1950s*, described a fourteen-year-old Irish girl called Mary in her book. After her father died and her mother's partner abused Mary, she ran away from home and took a boat. Within days of arriving in the East End, she was lured into prostitution and immediately fell pregnant. She delivered a baby at a home for mothers and babies run by the Catholic Church near London, but her baby was removed for adoption while Mary was asleep. This caused her to grow into a mentally disturbed young lady who eventually ended up in the British prison. This is not an isolated incident.

It was not just women who found life in Irish society intolerable. A large number of boys were abandoned by their parents, or raised by malicious relatives. With their unhappy childhood, they naturally harboured a grudge against Irish society.

It is impossible to provide exact figures but a substantial number of orphans, teenagers who were physically and mentally abused at Catholic-run institutions, asylums and industrial or residential schools, came to Britain during the post-war years. Some crossed the sea in order to make a fresh start anonymously, while others literally ran away. In many ways it was simply a matter of practicality to go to the nearest neighbouring country where there was ample work, as they needed to find a job in order to be independent.

The close relationship between the Catholic Church and the Irish State led to the Church's monopoly on social care and educational institutions, where thousands of children experienced physical, emotional and sexual abuse. These abuses, allegedly led to the most systemic human rights violations in the history of the State and occurred not just in Catholic institutions but also Protestant-run institutions such as Bethany Home in Dublin. Many of those children were – thankfully – able to leave those institutions at sixteen years old and fled to Britain to escape the memories of trauma they severely suffered as children. According to a report by the Commission to Inquire into Childhood Abuse in State Institutions in Ireland, also known as the Ryan Report (named after Justice Seán Ryan, who chaired the Commission), an estimated 30,000 or 37 per cent of survivors of these institutions from the 1920s to the 1980s were living in the UK by 2009.

Peter was one of the victims of institutional abuse who moved to London.

My life in Ireland wasn't so good. I was very, very badly treated by the brothers and nuns. I was an orphan; I didn't have a home life. I was working since I was six; waxing floors, that was my first job. My first home in Ireland was St Theresa's in Temple Hill, the Sisters of Charity in Blackrock, County Dublin ... When I got to the age of ten, they put me on the farm ... They taught me how to milk cows, instead of teaching me how to read and write ... The brothers [in St Augustine's, Obelisk Park where he stayed] were so very bad, they ill-treated you. They put injections in you. They used to kick you. If you weren't working fast enough: 'Can you move faster?' The beatings there were so bad. They used to take your trousers off and beat the arse out of you if you wet the bed.[13]

Ireland was relatively crime-free in the 1950s. This may have been due, in part, to certain sentencing practices by the courts that played role in divesting the State of undesirables or persons convicted of criminal offences.

Riordan noted: 'An Irishman with criminal aspirations almost invariably leaves this country and goes to England, sometimes voluntary, sometimes on the advice of the police, or even of a District Justice.'[14]

London, in particular proved to be an appealing refuge for criminals.

The other immigrant group worth noting are the Irish Travellers, who have also been coming to London to look for work for centuries. Their main occupations would have been chair canning, basket weavers, hawking, farm labourers, tin smiths, pot menders, entertainers and show men, amongst other professions.

Historically, fields at Seven Dials in Covent Garden and Gypsy Hill in Lambeth had a seasonal Travellers' community throughout the nineteenth century. During the post-war years, a record number of Travellers came to Britain to work and settled permanently. Mostly, they worked as labourers at the docks. Many men worked as traders at fares around London, also joining the building and construction trades throughout Britain.

Travellers also have had a long tradition of serving in the army. Their transient way of life, ability to improvise and adapt made them great soldiers. One of the most high-profile soldiers was Christy Joyce from Athlone, who won a couple of medals for bravery and dedication during the Second World War. He was invited to Buckingham Palace to receive his medals in person in 1946.

The majority of Irish Travellers seem to have been devout Catholics. According to a report by the Commission to Inquire into Child Abuse, children from the Travelling community often existed at Catholic institutions. Many of them, therefore also ended up moving to Britain.

2

BRITAIN

Are you crossing over? ... It won't be long till there's
nobody left here at all. They're all going. It won't be long
till I'll be crossing myself. Well, good luck to you.

Donall MacAmhlaigh[15]

Although Irish beggars were ordered to leave England in 1413 and
Irish vagrants were ordered to follow suit in 1629, prior to the 1841
Census, no official statistics exist regarding the number of Irish-born
residents in Britain as many of the Irish were considered not as settlers but transients, temporary workers or seasonal migrants. As the
flow of immigrants from Ireland continued, emigration to Britain had
become a well-established tradition by 1880.

It is always hard to determine the exact number of internal migrants.
For instance, no detailed information exists of the considerable movement of Scottish or Welsh people throughout England or within the
British Isles. As for the Irish, things are a little more complicated; since
the British Nationality Act of 1948, the Irish in the southern twenty-
six counties have ceased to be British subjects, although they still share
many of the rights and benefits granted to all British citizens.

The Commission on Emigration and other Population Problems
also found it impossible to produce reliable figures for gross post-war

emigration of the Irish, because of 'the difficulty of differentiating between emigrants and other travellers and of acquiring and maintaining continuous and accurate records of movements by sea and air'. In fact, many Irish people had been dividing their time between Britain and Ireland. They left initially for a short while as temporary or seasonal workers in Britain, and continued to return home on a regular basis. Due to this mobility of Irish people, they were often not showing up in the records.

Even during the post-war period, Irish people often worked for a certain period of time in Britain, returned home and then travelled back to Britain when necessary. Their mobility was not just physical but also reflected their psychological status. The Irish journalist T.P. O'Connor famously noted that the Irishman in Britain occupies a curious middle place between the nationality to which he belongs and the race among which he lives. Hence, they are neither fully Irish nor British.

ATTRACTIONS

The 1950s was a transition period for both Britain and Ireland. Unlike Ireland, it was a time of prosperity and economic growth for Britain. If you visit libraries and archives in England, you will notice that the documents and records of the 1950s are less extensive compared to other decades. It was a turbulent decade; everybody was busy finally getting on with their lives and focusing on regenerating the country after the war. It is also probable that the British Government was more meticulous about keeping records about the Irish before it became independent.[16] The post-war period of reconstruction in Britain attracted workers from many different Commonwealth countries, such as the West Indies and South Asia, as well as from Ireland. By the beginning of the 1960s there were almost a million Irish-born workers in England and Wales. The majority of Irish people in Britain were young and single.

Britain provided opportunities that simply did not exist in Ireland: Britain offered jobs that were not available back home; many future migrants had family members and friends already in Britain who helped the newcomers with jobs, accommodation and other useful information, leading to 'chain migration'; Britain offered higher living standards, better wages, a better life and a better status, especially for women; British cities provided an exciting city life and freedom that were not available in many, particularly rural, areas of Ireland; and British cities allowed Irish people to stay anonymously, which was perfectly suited for people with emotional and physical baggage to start a new life. Additionally, the relatively short distance from home made it easy – in terms of money and determination – for people to migrate, unlike leaving for far-flung corners of the world like America.

The generation of the 1950s was often referred as 'the lost generation', as it was a time when Irish immigration reached the highest levels since the aftermath of the Great Famine, approximately 100 years before. During this decade, around 500,000 Irish people left home, never to return permanently. The regions that suffered most from emigration were in the west of Ireland; the net emigration per annum in the 1950s was more than 40,000, or nearly 1 per cent of the population – the highest rate since the exceptional period in the 1880s.

IRISH STATUS IN BRITAIN

For centuries, Ireland and England have had a love-hate relationship. Irish historian R.F. Foster's book *Paddy and Mr Punch* describes it as follows:

Ireland strikes us as being the Prodigal Son of England, always going astray, then coming back, repenting and being forgiven. JOHN BULL may occasionally have been a harsh parent, but we are sure the old fellow

means well. It is too bad to see father and son at daggers drawn in
this way. When will Ireland be a good boy, and learn to remain quiet
at home?[17]

Ireland's historical connections and geographical proximity with
Britain are entwined. The Irish have traditionally been the most
numerous migrant workers in Britain, but have maintained their
own national and cultural identity. However, until 1922, Britain and
Ireland had been part of the same country for 120 years and were part
of a shared goods and labour market.

Britain has always treated Ireland as a special region, and Irish
people with a special status. After all, the Irish in Britain were techni-
cally not foreign immigrants in the sense of being complete strangers.
They were, and are, not totally alien to British religion, politics and
culture. Irish people are descended from invaders, conquerors and
settlers, just like Britain.

Despite the fact that the Irish Free State was neutral during the
Second World War, nearly 5,000 Irish people joined the British Army
as soldiers to fight on the front line, 120,000 Irish people worked for
the Army, and another 170,000 took up jobs in the war economy in
Britain, even though the British Government somewhat restricted
immigration from Ireland during the war.

In 1949, the Irish Free State became the Republic of Ireland and
left the Commonwealth. However, under the Ireland Act 1949, the
British Parliament, it confirmed that the Republic of Ireland was
not a foreign country in British law. Britain continued to treat Irish
citizens no differently to its own citizens and in fact gave Irish immigrants a special status while in Britain. They could freely enter Britain
to work, settle, vote, and even claim social security benefits, although
many British people who worked at the benefit office and the majority of Irish people were not aware of this. During the time when the
war-damaged nation needed to be rebuilt, the British Government
heavily relied on the Irish labour force and so the law readily enabled
them to hold a job in the British market.

Despite their importance to the economy, Irish people's invisibility in Britain is well documented and researched. In theory, the Irish were treated just like British citizens. However, being excluded from controls on entry and entitled to various rights upon arrival directly contributed to their unseen status. Their cultural difference has long been ignored, because they are a white and British Isles population group.

For instance, when Britain was suffering from a severe housing shortage during the time when the number of immigrants coming to Britain from Commonwealth countries grew rapidly, the Irish – although they struggled to find a place to live just like other immigrants – did not get the help they much needed from the British Government, because the Irish were not officially recognised as a minority ethnic group who needed support.

Even though the Irish were de facto British citizens, they were relatively poorly paid, just like other immigrants typically working for the NHS, London Transport Executive and British Rail, amongst other companies. Although the Irish didn't fall into a Commonwealth immigrant category, they suffered from prejudice and racism, just like West Indians and Asians from Commonwealth countries. With the same skin colour, the Irish didn't look any different from the British and were generally regarded as British, but this did not prevent their deprived positions going unnoticed by many.

Despite the poverty faced by a great deal of Irish citizens, some did manage to integrate effortlessly and relatively quickly into the British way of life, as they had been doing for centuries. Because of their shared history and common heritage, the Irish and the British had profound influence on each other.

Newcomers often used their family networks and friends, or even county associations in order that they survive the initial adjustment period relatively hassle-free.

Many Irish people had relatives and friends who had migrated to Britain from the Great Depression period onwards; these contacts regularly wrote letters and sent money back to Ireland.

Consequently, those already living and thriving in Britain provided
fares for the next to follow. As the path was already paved, almost as
a matter of course, many immigrants did not even look for a suitable
job or a place to live.

A press photographer named Paddy Fahey recorded the Irish community in London in the late 1940s and '50s. He described the life
of a typical immigrant: 'An Irish man would return home annually
and he would bring back the first cousin or a younger brother. And it
went on. The next year he goes over. One family living in Kilburn –
there were nine brothers.'[18]

The people in Ireland all knew what it was like to be in London,
through letters and holiday visits of emigrants. As a result, chain
migration had become institutionalised and a part of the generally
accepted pattern of life.

After losing his job at Clover Meat in County Waterford, Jim
Duggan decided to leave Ireland:

> I came to London because my brother was living in Tufnell Park
> [North London]. I also had a couple of good friends living in the
> same area. I had no choice but to leave for London to make a living
> because unemployment in Ireland was awful at that time and I was
> married with kids.[19]

Sometimes only elderly people remained in certain localities, as the
children and youngsters had gone to England or elsewhere. Donall
MacAmhlaigh from Galway wrote a book about his life as a navvy in
the 1950s England. He once visited home in Galway during Easter:
'I ate a fine Irish dinner: bacon, cabbage, roast and boiled potatoes
with a nice sweet to follow. I was the only one of the family present.
Kevin is in Daventry, Noel in Hampshire, Brian in Sussex and
Dympna, our only sister, in London.'[20]

The rural Irish typically didn't move to Dublin but preferred to
move to large urban cities abroad in which the Irish had already
formed communities. The majority of households in rural Ireland had

more affinity with and knowledge of London, Liverpool, New York, Boston or Glasgow than Dublin.

Positive impressions of London or other foreign cities by successful emigrants were repeatedly passed on through letters, holiday visits and nothing but favourable newspaper articles. Irish people typically came back home looking rather sophisticated and nicely dressed and those 'city people' did little to discourage others from following. Especially for young girls and boys, life in London or other British cities appeared extremely attractive. Social freedom and ample entertainment options such as the cinema, dancehalls, music and fashion were tremendous deciding factors to migrate. With the existing network, it didn't take immense courage to embark on a new journey; many youngsters, therefore, were rather keen to follow their friends and relatives.

WORKING IN BRITAIN

According to data from the International Labour Organisation, in three industries – building and construction, engineering, and printing and publishing – the wages in Ireland were relatively higher than British wages between 1926 and the mid-1980s, apart from the period 1952-1964, when Irish wages collapsed. During the Second World War, Irish wage levels had fallen considerably behind those in Britain due to poor economic performance; throughout the 1950s, the average income in Ireland was just half of that in Britain. Furthermore, the British economy played an important role in determining Irish wages. The average UK annual salary was just over £100 in 1950, and the average weekly wage in 1957 was £10. The majority of Irish people were clearly attracted to the higher wages in Britain.

Work conditions significantly improved in Britain after the war. In the late 1940s, the typical manual labourer in Britain was entitled to only one week's paid holiday a year. It was only after the Second

World War that it became the norm to work five days a week rather than six days. It is estimated that around 70 per cent of workers were in manual labour in the 1950s.

Apart from higher wages, Irish workers, especially the women, found that they received better treatment. Just like domestic workers got better status in Britain, according to Louie Bennett of the Irish Women Workers' Union, the treatment received by the women who worked in British factories was 'a thousand times better'; British employers were more focused on work conditions such as hours, remuneration and environment.

Many Irish politicians' attitudes toward emigration was coldly pragmatic – 'let them go; they will come back with money'. Emigration had not just become a massive, relentless and efficiently managed national enterprise; according to Paddy Lynch, an adviser to the first inter-party government, it apparently 'allowed those at home to maintain their standard of living'. Irish politicians all acknowledged that. The Irish typically did not come home unless they had money and success stories to tell. As migration is a leit-motif of Irish life, all Irish abroad sent money back home as if they were born to do so. Many children in Ireland were traditionally brought up for emigration to fund further emigration and provide remittances for their parents, siblings and other family members to make a living.

A Donegal man, Patrick MacGill, worked as a navvy in Scotland and eventually became a journalist and writer, publishing his auto-biographical novel entitled *Children of the Dead End*. He articulated his bitter sentiments and how he felt about it in details in his book: 'I was born and bread merely to support my parents ... I was merely brought into the world to support those who were responsible for my existence.'[21]

As a young teenager, MacGill knew that he missed out on being a child because of his responsibility to earning cash. He felt the unfair-ness of life but tried to accept what was considered the right thing to do:

I thought it would be so fine to have all my wages to myself to spend in the shops, to buy candy just like a little boy or to take a ride on the swing-boats or merry-go-rounds at the far corner of the market-place. I would like to do those things, but the voice of conscience reproved me for even thinking of them.[22]

In 1951, remittances amounted to £10 million and formed 2.5 per cent of the total national income, according to the Central Statistics Office. Between 1939 and 1969, £2.2 billion was sent privately to Ireland in the form of telegrams, or wire and money orders from Britain alone.

As Irish people religiously sent money home, their remittances kept not just the whole family, but the entire country going. But in order to save money, a vast majority of them sacrificed their lives as they suffered social and economic consequences of appalling working conditions and an impoverished lifestyle. An immigrant described:

I was always savin' [*sic*] so much a week at that time. Every decent Irishman sent so much home at that time; whether you wanted to or not, it was expected of you. You didn't even think what they were doin' [*sic*] with it at home … You felt good about it; it was a bit of a religion, sort of thing.[23]

Most families with a relative working abroad had their incomes increased, but as receiving remittances became a norm, some people merely became accustomed to receive it without understanding how hard migrant workers had to work to earn it and did not show much appreciation.

Then after a while, you realised they didn't really require your money at all, and you stopped sendin' [*sic*] it, when you got to about twenty-seven or twenty-eight. All they were doin' [*sic*] with it was putting' [*sic*] it in the bank themselves, or the post office. A married man would be different, obviously... A strange life, but the women back in Ireland, and the men over there, just took it for granted – they didn't feel anything odd about it.[24]

Deprived of life, the migrant workers who had to leave home and work from an early age eventually became disillusioned due to the injustices they had no choice but to endure. Typical Irish workers abroad received very similar letters from home:

My mother sent me a letter that another brother was born to me – the second since I left home – and asking me for some more money to help them along with the rent. But my disposition was changing; my outlook on life was becoming bitter, and I hated to be slave to farmers, landlords, parents, and brothers and sisters. Every new arrival into the family was reported to me as something for which I should be grateful. 'Send home some more money, you have another brother,' ran the letters, and a sense of unfairness crept over me. The younger members of the family were taking the very life-blood out of my veins, and on account of them I had to suffer kicks, snubs, cold and hunger. New brothers and sisters were no pleasure to me. I rebelled against the imposition and did not answer the letter.[25]

HARSH REALITIES

One of the most visible downsides of life in Britain was racism. The Irish have traditionally been subject to oppression and discrimination, and the racism and the conditions that the Irish community face today are deeply rooted in British colonial history. Anti-Irish or Anti-Catholic racism in Britain originated during the reign of Henry II. English-born Pope Adrian IV gave Henry permission to conquer Ireland in order to strengthen the papacy's control over the Irish Church in 1155. The Anglo-Norman Invasion of Ireland began in 1169, and it is profoundly associated with the colonisation of Ireland.

For centuries, London in particular has been a magnet not only for the Irish, but other foreign workers and settlers, and Britain is used to dealing with newcomers. But during the post-war period, when foreigners arrived in such large numbers simultaneously and were taking certain jobs from local workers – even though these were jobs that locals refused to do – growing antagonism against immigrants exploded.

One of the major racial incidents was the Notting Hill race riots, which occurred in west London over several nights in late August and early September 1958. The Notting Hill racial attacks started when a group of white youths confronted a Swedish woman, who was arguing with her Jamaican husband at Latimer Road tube station. Although not strictly Irish-related, this incident highlighted the tension between immigrants and local white population.

Although depending on circumstances and background such as age, employment and place of residence, average Irish people typically experienced some sort of prejudice or discrimination. Patrick MacGill recalled his feelings when he started working in Britain: 'I felt that I was a man classed among swine, and that is a very bitter truth to learn at eighteen.'

After the influx of Commonwealth immigrants, however, their status became tricky. In some cases, things got better, while others remained the same. Although the Irish and other foreign workers did the jobs that no local people would take, some British people believed that migrant workers as a whole were taking jobs away from working-class people; they were seen as a threat to the local workers, a pool of cheap labour that suppressed wages. The majority of Irish immigrants in Britain happened to belong to the working class and much of the discrimination that occurred was based on class rather than nationality. In an attempt to fit in, a few people with obvious Irish names changed them to more British-sounding names during this period. For instance, Seán O'Neal simply became

John Neal. Others made an effort to loose their Irish brogue and adapt a British accent or to refrain from speaking when looking for accommodation so that no one could tell that they were Irish.

Being Catholic was not easy in 1950s London. The conflict in Northern Ireland was getting serious and Irish people generally had to keep their heads down. This Irish girl's experience was not an isolated incident:

> It was hard to find work as a Catholic, because when I went for an interview the first question that they asked was what Church you went to. Another girl that went to school with me, and her marks weren't anything like mine, applied for the same job as me. She was a Protestant and she got it.[26]

During the 1950s, reports of attacks on the Catholic Church and its people frequently appeared in the media. Anti-religious talks were common at workplaces. Concerned Irish priests regularly came to London and gave advice on how to deal with discrimination, prejudice and attacks. On such occasions, the church was typically packed, proving the seriousness of the situation.

Two Dublin Jesuits came to the Church of Our Lady of Willesden in October 1952 to give a talk on how to deal with the issue. About 1,500 people turned up and after the service parishioners received a copy of the campaign textbook called *Handy Answers*.

While there were jobs for all, finding accommodation was a different story. During the 1950s, many landlords and owners of B&Bs and other boarding houses – especially in London and some other British cities – put signs reading 'No Blacks, No Irish, No Dogs'. Another version, found in areas where there were no black residents, read 'Vacancies Available – Irish Need Not Apply'. In Scotland where there were no black workers, but plenty of Irish migrant workers, the notice was simply worded 'No Catholics'.

British politicians, for some reason, assumed that foreign workers would not stay too long in Britain. During a discussion on the role of 'colonial workers', MP Harold Davies stated: 'Having helped our productivity and output, that manpower or woman power could go back to the colonies and be a nucleus of productivity there.'

Aneurin Bevan, then Minister of Health, admitted that housing was one of the least successful aspects of the new Welfare State up until 1951, while he was busy setting up the National Health Service.

Housing was the most conspicuous sign of inequality. Racial and social identity, income and status were linked to the kind of housing in which people lived. Upon arrival, many Irish people were genuinely shocked to discover just how prevalent anti-Irish sentiment was in England. Anecdotes on how difficult it was to find a place to live are abundant:

I remember coming across from Ireland to England in 1953, as a nervous and frightened nineteen-year-old. Work was very easy to find but accommodation was a different matter.[27]

My family arrived in England from Dublin in 1958. Like most Irish immigrants, my parents came over to find good jobs and to improve future prospects for their children … 'No Wogs, No Dogs, No Irish' became a familiar sight, pinned to B & B front doors. My parents suffered many an insult. I don't know how they coped.[28]

Wherever you went, nobody wanted the Irish. If the landlord heard you speaking, heard your accent, then the place was suddenly 'gone' – already let.[29]

They were alright – a bit prejudiced you know. You'd look for a room and they'd say 'Oh, that room was taken yesterday,' something like that. 'Why didn't you take down the notice then?' Their reply was 'Don't you speak to me like that, this is England.' 'Go stuff yourself,' I'd say.[30]

Irish navvies suffered from a negative reputation in Britain and had to endure discrimination despite their hard work. Many assumed that

they were loud, drunk, and frequently covered in mud and dirt. Some
Irish people, however, felt that certain young and reckless navvies
behaved badly and got what they deserved: 'In the 1950s, they were
bloody disgrace, young chaps fighting, abusing passersby, grabbing
girls in the arse – this was my impression. They were uneducated
labourers who liked their Guinness.'[31]

   While it was true that some of the young men behaved badly,
in numerous cases, British people were merely being ignorant in
believing that all Irishmen were drunk and dirty navvies, and should
be avoided. Tony from County Cork came to London aged 19
in 1955. He ignored the card in the window and secured a room
intended for rent to non-Irish people.

> There was this lovely little semi-Victorian house, and there was a
> card 'rooms to let'. The woman who opened the door was wearing a
> long black dress and a bonnet. Her husband worked as a tax inspector
> and they decided to supplement income by letting rooms. She let me
> into the house and I had a cup of tea and biscuits with her. At 6pm,
> Rodney, her husband came back. He was an English gentleman.
> He asked me, 'You are Irish, aren't you?' And his wife Carol asked
> me, 'Are you Irish?' and I said, 'Yes.' But she said to her husband, 'He
> is such a nice fellow. It is up to you, I don't mind.' I was in the house
> although the card says 'No Irish'. The image of the Irish was covered
> in mud and dirt, wearing Wellingtons, a donkey jacket, coming back
> late and probably getting pissed. The British believed the Irish were
> an unwelcomed bunch.[32]

Seán Nunan, then secretary of the Department of External Affairs,
acknowledged the appalling conditions in which Irish immigrants,
especially navvies, were living. As a consequence, the Irish clergy
showed great interest in housing for Irish immigrants in London,
although their view did not often correspond with that of the Irish
Government. According to Nunan, an Irish priest expressed great
satisfaction, saying that he was content to know 150 immigrant

men living in three small houses near Southwark Cathedral. The houses were obviously packed but the landlord was Catholic and the cathedral was nearby. Rather than living in an English – or pagan as they called it – household in a better condition, the clergy firmly believed that an Irish environment would be best, to preserve religion.

Various religious and other charities helped and opened residential houses for disadvantaged Irish people. One of the earliest hostels for Irish workers was the Residential House for Irish workers in Tollington Park, North London. Fr George Groves set up this hostel and, since this was considered a somewhat momentous achievement, Cardinal Griffin officially opened it. Cardinal Griffin believed that the large number of Irish workers coming to a non-Catholic country with few contacts and little experience of life needed a support system, as 'conditions over here are very different from those in which the boys have been brought up'.

Young Irishmen could come to this hostel immediately on arrival in London and stay for a time while they sought proper lodgings and a job, as well as adjusting to a new environment. Most importantly, residents would receive guidance and advice from resident priests. Even before crossing the ocean, soon-to-be migrant workers received the address of this hostel so that priests in Ireland would have less difficulty in advising them upon departure.

Another organisation that assisted in making temporary lodging arrangements was The Irish Priests' Committee, which was formed in 1950 in the Westminster, Southwark and Brentwood dioceses. A lay group notably trained by the committee met newly arrived Irish migrants at Euston and Paddington railway stations and provided assistance. Furthermore, this versatile group set up a fund for a large social, cultural and recreational centre for Irish people in London.

Gerard clearly remembers that Irish people had a difficult time:

> There was a big wave of emigration from Ireland in the 1950s. I think it was partly because the labour market suddenly opened up here.

There were a lot of employment opportunities. A new government
came in power in 1945 and the recovery from the war was still going
on – I can still remember quite clearly the signs of the 'No Irish, No
Blacks, No Dogs' on the shop windows. Irish people really did have
a hard time.[33]

Another Irish resident recounted their experience of pubs: 'If you
went into a pub with an Irish accent, they were reluctant to serve
you. The English felt superior; that's the way they were brought
up.'[34]

Some experienced prejudice at work, too. Anne O'Neill, a ticket
collector for London Transport, recalled an unpleasant incident:

> I remember one day when I was getting abuse on the bus and this
> other passenger intervened. He said to the guy who was abusing me,
> 'Oi, you – would you do this girl's job?' 'No,' says your man. 'Right
> then, leave her alone. If you're not prepared to do her job, and I'm
> not prepared to do her job, leave her alone. We're Englishmen,' he said,
> 'white-collar men'.[35]

A migrant worker who worked 'on the belt' in Schweppes also received
some offensive comments:

> We were working with English girls – they were all English except for
> myself and my friend Maureen. The others used to be always saying that
> we weren't doing it right and they used to pick on us a lot. They used to
> say, 'You Irish you don't know how to do it properly,' or 'What are you
> doing here?' They'd make some nasty comments or other.[36]

Quite a few people were lucky to find the right landlord or landlady.
Tony's experience was not uncommon:

> I came to London from Fishguard harbour through Wales. I got off
> the train at Paddington station and as I walked 50 steps, there was

a fellow with a familiar Cork accent. There were 17 or 18 porters from Ireland working there. Cork porters are easily recognisable with their flat accent. They said to me, 'Come here boy, what are you doing? Anywhere to go?' I said, 'No'. And one of the guys said, 'Why don't you go to the end of this road. There is a café and wait for me.' I went there and I had a nice cup of tea and cake. And later, we went down to Harrow Road. There was a lady, a local fixer, accommodation lady. She was English. I met this woman and ended up in a room sharing with three other single beds in it. The rent was £17 a month. I had two companions – Irish navvies or sub-contractors from Mayo. They were older than me. There were awful lot of young Irish men died as a result of the way they lived. They drunk too much, they ate too much greasy stuff – black pudding, sausages, chips, etc … Anyway, so I landed on Harrow Road. I had holiday money about £30 in my pocket. We could make about £7 a week at that time.[37]

The post-war era was often referred to as a decade of transition when old standards had vanished. One of the downsides of this economically booming period was the increasing crime. In the 1950s, for instance, up to 6,000 crimes a year occurred only in Hammersmith, west London, and fewer than thirteen detectives attempted to solve them.

After the Second World War, youth delinquency became a visible problem amongst Irish people; evidence shows that there was a high proportion of young Catholic people turning up at juvenile courts. The *Catholic Herald* covered all kinds of incidents throughout the decade. The chairman of the Children's Committee of London County Council pointed out that 30 per cent of children in their care were Catholics.

Ruth Morrah, chairman of the London Juvenile Courts, noted that priests and nuns did not come to court to give information about the children brought before her, but often sent along someone who barely knew about them. The *Catholic Herald* reported that an assistant prison governor found that Catholic boys 'are appallingly ignorant of their religion and as delinquents, they are in no way different to non-Catholics, and added the Irish boy were a particular problem as 'he lacked the wit and sophisticated air of the English boy'.

Sister Catherine, headmistress at Burnt Oak Secondary Modern School, noted that children were potential delinquents around the age when the mother went back to work. She suggested that schools should be open at night for those children who had to look after themselves at home.

Between 1950 and 1961, the contribution of the Irish to violent crime in London rose from 9.7 per cent to 12.2 per cent. In the same decade, Irish-born immigrants from the Republic counted for 12 per cent of the prison population in England, Wales and Scotland. A study estimated that in 1960, approximately 3,000 Irish-born males were imprisoned in English and Welsh prisons compared to 1,700 comparable committals to prisons in the Republic of Ireland.[38] Some research suggests that many Irish men were incarcerated in Pentonville Prison, North London.

There is no doubt that the British police targeted the new immigrants, but perhaps it was with good reason; the upsurge in criminal offences by Irish immigrants was evident.

Irish migration to Britain during this period was essentially driven by higher wages and this brought a new-found wealth and increasing disposable income.[39] What's more, young Irish migrants to Britain experienced the freedom of being away from home, freed from the constraining influence of family and neighbours, for the first time. The influence of religious or clerical control in Ireland was significantly stronger, particularly during this period, and alcohol more freely available; the use of alcohol seems to be a particularly strong feature in criminal offending by Irish immigrants as identified by senior English police officers during this period.

Ironically, the drop in the crime rate and the prison population in Ireland paralleled vast outflows of emigrants from Ireland to mainly

Britain. Crime rates in the Republic of Ireland fell to an all-time low in the late 1950s and the daily average prison and borstal population fell below 400 in 1958. As a result, the Irish Government began to close down prisons.[40]

Unfortunately, while the majority of women did remarkably well in Britain, a few were not as fortunate. It is impossible to calculate the exact numbers due to the nature of the business, but it is believed that Irishwomen made up one of the highest percentage of prostitutes working on the streets of London. It wasn't hard to spot Irish girls on the streets of London. A male immigrant noted:

> Perhaps they would have gone that way even at home, but they ended up on the streets. I remember speaking to one of the girls and telling her I was going back home on holidays. She gave me money and asked me to give it to her father. 'Tell him I'm working for Walls,' was what she said. 'Don't tell him what I'm doing.' And that was sad. Very sad. There was no support for those girls, same as with the Irish navvy.[41]

The Legion of Mary was one of the institutions that rescued count-less women from prostitution. The Catholic girls typically lost their faith once they started working on the streets and were unlikely to return to church. The primary aim of the Legion of Mary was to get them back into practicing their faith, to get in touch with the priest and to encourage them to go to confession. Having been persuaded, some girls were placed in convents to be rehabilitated, while some lucky girls eventually found a conventional job or even a husband.

An article in the *Catholic Herald* on 4 October 1957 reported that there were more than thirty women legionaries engaged in rescue work in London. What they did was to talk to girls on the street. Sometimes the girls admitted that they were Catholics, while others stopped the conversation as soon as the legionaries explained their purpose. The area they covered included notorious stretches of the

West End area, such as Soho. Their persistent and courageous work was not limited to London; they also worked further afield, in cities such as Manchester, Birmingham, Liverpool and Cardiff, where newly arrived Irish immigrants were lured into the trade.

Overwhelmed by the large number of women on the street, the Legions in London appealed for help in newspaper articles in 1957 in a desperate attempt to recruit more women to help in getting prostitutes off the streets. They were also in urgent need of accommodation in which rescued girls could stay for a night or two while they tried to figure out their next move.

The Legion of Mary sometimes had to act as a next of kin. Due to the nature of work, prostitutes often failed to form any long-term relationships or even normal friendships. Consequently, when they were ill or dying, they had no one to talk to and the local legionaries were the last resort and the only lifeline. The Legion of Mary often received urgent calls from hospitals informing them that women they had rescued once in the past were dying.

LONDON LIFE

London has been a magnet for all foreign settlers, immigrants and migrant workers since the seventeenth century. Throughout history, especially since medieval times, there have been Irish settlements in Britain. Irish people have been numerous, scattered throughout all facets of life, from the upper class to the working class such as landlords, priests, politicians, lawyers, actors, artists, writers, builders, shoe repairmen, porters, factory workers, milk-sellers and all kinds of street workers.

During the Victorian period, a steady flow of Irish migrants settled in London. At one point, they made up approximately 20 per cent of London's population. One of the most visible settlements was in east London, where Irish immigrants tried to make their living as dock workers. By 1870, there were more Irish people in London than in Dublin. As the Irish had been living in the worst slum districts of

British cities, the terms 'ghetto' and 'colony' had been frequently associated with an Irish presence. The first well-known 'Irish colony' in London was at St Giles, just off Oxford Street; the major thoroughfare in the city centre.

By the 1950s, things had improved immensely compared with the post-Famine and general Victorian periods. Their ubiquitous presence in London made it extremely difficult to pinpoint where most of them lived but the most densely concentrated areas were Kilburn, the districts around Euston and Camden stations, Hammersmith, the South Bank, Elephant and Castle and the Docklands.

According to the 1951 British census, over one-third of Irish emigrants in England and Wales were living in the Greater London area. The number of Irish immigrants in Greater London was 8,193,921 with 3,347,982 in central London. 3.3 per cent of the administrative county of London was Irish-born, the percentage in Paddington was 8.4 per cent and eight other boroughs had more than 5 per cent of their population who were born in Ireland.[42]

The number of Irish-born residents in London rose by more than half between 1951 and 1961 to reach a total of 172,493. The Irish-born population of London constituted 5.4 per cent of the total.[43] Camden was a popular area to live in because it is close to Euston station; the last stop of the Irish mail train from Holyhead. Many lodging houses and hostels for Irish construction workers existed near building sites.

Arriving in London from a rural village in Ireland was a tremendous shock to some. One immigrant pointed out 'I didn't see a single person with threadbare clothes or worn-out footwear. Clothes and much else are dearer here than in Ireland and I'm thinking that I'd be well advised to go home to Ireland once a year and fit myself out.'[44]

The Irish have been an integral part of the city, not just as a valuable workforce, but as part of the process of forming the city's cultural identity. Some of them worked in the metropolis temporarily but on a regular basis, while the others settled, had children who typically became British and formed a prominent community.

By the 1950s, the service sector accounted for half of London's economy, while the manufacturing sector comprised 42 per cent. Scores of manufacturing firms were established and flourished, principally those that produced consumer goods such as televisions, washing machines and radios, as owning these goods became increasingly common. Only 4.3 per cent of homes had television sets in 1950, but by 1956, the figure was nearly 50 per cent.[45]

The office work boom brought more than 50,000 new white-collar jobs and there was a large demand for female typists, secretaries and general office workers. Women benefited most from this surge in employment opportunities and they outnumbered men in London's offices during the 1950s. The number of mothers in employment in London had tripled.

Although rationing and reconstruction were still ongoing at the beginning of the 1950s in London, it was a decade of societal change and prosperity. Many new trends were embraced, such as consumer culture, American values, fashion and music like rock 'n' roll. Record quantities of imports and exports entered through London's docks.

Ultimately, there was no place like London. For the newly arrived immigrants, this was very much an Irish city. One new resident noted: 'This town is more Irish than most of the places back home … the Irish in London … have a great life, plenty of their own people around them, galore Irish dances and somewhere to go every night of the week.[46]

Irish people summed up their impression of London in typically honest fashion: 'There are too many opportunities for spending and I'd never save a single penny.'[47]

There was no shortage of entertainment and fun in London. A popular pastime among the Irish population was visiting Speaker's Corner in Hyde Park, where people discussed and debated all sorts of subjects in an autonomous and laid-back manner. Hundreds of thousands of Irish people spontaneously gathered at the corner as they strove for the freedom of speech and expression. Jim Duggan, a trade unionist, from County Waterford, said that he went to speakers' corner with his friends every weekend.[48]

There was also an extensive protest march in 1956 through Hyde Park to the Irish Embassy, petitioning for the release of Republican prisoners. Hyde Park was also the location where Passionist Fathers annually conducted the mediation on the Stations of the Cross from the Catholic Evidence Guild platform on Good Friday.

To the majority of working people, the weekend meant a washing day, much of which was undertaken at public baths and laundries. In the 1950s, a couple of these venues existed in London, which provided local people with a place to bathe and wash their clothes.

The first public washhouse in Britain was opened on Frederick Street, Liverpool in 1842. Kitty Wilkinson, an Irish immigrant who was the wife of a labourer, opened it to clean countless clothes by using bleach, or chloride of lime, at a charge of 1*d* per week during the cholera epidemic. Initially a destitute immigrant from Ireland, Kitty and her mother worked as domestic servants in England. By opening the public washhouse, she saved hundreds of thousands of lives and later became known as the Saint of the Slums. She was one of the most remarkable Irish immigrants in Britain.

The first public baths in London were opened at Goulston Square in Whitechapel in 1847. After the Second World War, new houses were commonly built with bathrooms, but a great number of families were still living in old Victorian houses with a shared bathroom or no bathroom at all. For the majority of people in London, the act of having a bath was something of a luxury, since most of them were not even able to fill a tin bath in front of the fire.

Typical public baths provided enclosed cabins, each with a seat, a hook and a mirror, while the washhouse offered large tubs, mangles and driers. Public baths and washhouses were also used as a place to socialise, especially for women who tended to stay there longer than men.

Jim Duggan recalled a local public baths: 'There was a public bath and washhouse in Kentish Town. We used to have a good wash once a week. There were about twenty small bathrooms and it was six pennies for thirty minutes. My wife was washing clothes there as well.'[49]

Another popular leisure activity was visiting theatres. London was, and remains, a city of arts – an international hub of theatre and publishing, and the most popular destination for Irish writers and artists. Even in the 1950s, the London's West End and other areas in London provided ample theatres, and various shows and performances were available every day. Many Irish theatre lovers flocked to the Embassy Theatre on Eaton Avenue in Swiss Cottage. The theatre was established in 1928, and a school of acting was opened in the theatre in 1932. After the war, in particular, the theatre became very popular as it produced many Irish plays and is widely considered to have a long record of Irish theatrical success. Some of the notable Irish productions included *Red Roses for Me* by Sean O'Casey and *They Got What They Wanted* by Louis Dalton.

The Watergate Theatre near Charing Cross also showed various Irish plays and was a popular venue for the Irish to visit. Another theatres also popular amongst the Irish in West End were the Stoll Theatre on Portugal Street and the Gaiety Theatre, both around Aldwych.

In response to huge demand, Irish newspapers were easily available in London. Some of the most popular newspapers included the *Kerryman*, the *Connacht Tribune*, the *Anglo-Celt*, the *Cork Examiner*, the *United Irishman*, the *Irish Democrat*, and a paper in Irish: *Amárach*, or *Tomorrow*. The *Irish Independent* had a London bureau on Fleet Street and its London correspondents covered daily articles from the British capital as well as writing stories for the regular column called 'London Letter'. Journalists covering Irish affairs attended extensive Irish events and functions – the majority of which were entertainment-related – every single day.

Fr Seamus Fullam, who worked with the Irish in London, identified culture shock as the main difficulty facing young Irish immigrants on their arrival in Britain.[50] For instance, the majority of newcomers did not even understand the British accent at all upon arrival. But most of them soon adapted themselves relatively well to their new surroundings and enjoyed the city life which offered them not just secure jobs and steady income, but freedom and self-esteem.

3

MIGRANTS AT WORK

We'll lift our time and go, lads, the long road lies before,
The places that we know, lads, will know our like no more.
Foot forth! The last bob's paid out, some see their last shift through,
But the men who are not played out, have other jobs to do.[51]

Patrick MacGill

The Second World War caused tremendous damage to British infrastructure, and £7 billion – approximately a quarter of the country's national wealth – was spent on recovery and regeneration. Following the end of the war, the government launched a major reconstruction effort, but there was still plenty of work to do in order to rebuild the country.

During this period of rapid expansion in the British economy, a considerable number of skilled and unskilled workers were necessary. They were actively and openly recruited from Ireland, as well as Commonwealth countries, to build infrastructure and to work in hospitals, hotels, offices and factories.

Immediately after the war, London faced a housing crisis as many homes were destroyed and damaged in the war. The British Government decided on building high-rise tower blocks of flats as a way to solve this housing shortage problem.

According to the Commission on Emigration, when leaving Ireland for Britain after the Second World War, Irish people had to fill in their travel documents and provide their occupational status. Approximately three-quarters of men described their last occupation as that of unskilled labourers, builders' labourers or agricultural workers, while more than half of their female counterparts described themselves as domestic servants. This suggests that the majority generally lacked training, education or any qualifications or previous occupation, although some professional people may have been forced to take manual jobs. Unskilled men in particular arrived without cash or pre-arranged work, but work was abundant. John Hurley from Cork, who came to work in London after the war, said: 'In those days, it was commonly said there were plenty of jobs for all as long as you can stand on your own two feet'.

In contrast, female migrant workers were mostly recruited through employment agencies or independently, and managed to secure a job and accommodation before they left Ireland.

NAVVIES

The most overwhelming and quintessential image of Irish male workers in Britain was the navvy. According to the Collins dictionary, a navvy is a person employed to do hard physical work, such as road and canal building. It is an abbreviation of navigator, the first of whom built the first navigation canals in the eighteenth century. Through the course of history, the Irish navvies have contributed enormously to the British economy and helped build its infrastructure. They have been involved with all sorts of construction projects such as canals, roads and railways all across the country, providing the most essential and indispensable labour force in the process of developing the country.

Work was extremely hard; one navvy and recalled his first day: 'I was ready to fall by the time the dinner break came and only half the day was gone by then.'

Ubiquitous Irish navvies were described as follows:

> The construction industry was traditionally the largest single employer
> of Irish male emigrants to Britain, predominantly men coming from
> the West of Ireland, and in the early post-war period the image of the
> 'all-brawn, no brain navvy' became almost the predominant negative
> stereotype of the Irish in Britain – not alone for the British but even
> for many of the Irish back home.[52]

The Crown in Cricklewood, North London was originally established in the 1750s and was rebuilt in 1889. During the 1950s, this
lodging house and pub became one of the best known and essential
meeting spots for the rapidly growing Irish community that lived
into the area, approximately 3 miles from Camden Town. It was
common to see Irish workers standing in front of the Crown in the
early morning, waiting to be picked up for casual work.

Apart from this pub, there were various pick-up spots and
streets such as in Cricklewood Broadway, Kilburn High Road,
Holloway Road, Camden High Street, Elephant and Castle,
and Hammersmith. After being picked up by vans and trucks, they
would be scattered to various construction sites.

> In those days, they got picked up off the street and worked on the
> lump. The chap would announce – 'I want 60 men' in Cricklewood
> Broadway and they would jump on the truck. At the end of the day,
> they got paid cash-in-hand. Most Irish men were not very literate
> or professionals, so they were doing construction work, going into
> buildings. If you are prepared, there were plenty of jobs and there was
> no need to be anyone to be out of work.[53]

When picking workers, the first thing the ganger man or agent would
look at was the working boots:

... if the boots were damp or a smear of concrete on them, there was a greater chance of a job because they had been working the previous day.[54]

A former navvy recalled how jobs were abundant in Camden Town:

Before I ever left home, I knew all you had to do was go to Camden Town and you'd get work. Just pick a colour – whatever colour van you liked. There'd be thousands of men there every morning. If you weren't there between half six and quarter to seven, there wouldn't be a wagon left.[55]

John Leonard was a navvy from Donegal, who came to London via Scotland. With his experience of working as a tunneller, he came down to London with a bunch of fellow Irishmen to work on the London Underground, when the Victoria line was being built. His experience was typical of many navvies:

I was mining with a spade until they introduced the digger shields. When the shields came in, conditions improved. It was all conveyor belts and no digging. All you had to do was build the segments. You had a winch and wire band which you'd fit around the segment. You worked in a five-man gang. There was a leading miner, two miners and two miner's labourers. I was a labourer at first, for a year or so, and then a miner. I worked all over the Victoria line, not with the same men all the time. Each section of work would have a price based on an estimate of how much work was required and how much time. If the price didn't suit the gang, you might split up, move to another gang on some other part of the line. I remember the work as very hard. At first you had twelve-hour shifts though there were breaks where you had to come up to the surface and tea was sent down when they brought in the shields. It was three eight-hour shifts, a day shift from 7 o'clock to 3 o'clock, an afternoon or back shift from 3 o'clock to 11 o'clock, then the night shift from 11 o'clock to 7 o'clock. There were a lot of injuries but usually nothing serious and there was only one man killed on the Victoria line. The skips carrying the muck used to come off the tracks and someone would break a leg or lose a finger. But I wouldn't call it really dangerous and I never hurt myself. You worked a five-day week and had Saturday and Sunday off. If you were on the night shift, Monday night you could be out until late on a Sunday night and then sleep all day on the Monday. The men would go out drinking and dancing together, and also to the Irish Centre for Mass. Some of the men were cousins, some I went to school with.[56]

The Irish navvies were often favoured over the British. This was not only because they were easily available, but it seemed like they have distinguished qualities that British navvies didn't have. A Birmingham employer gave evidence on the Irish navvy in 1836:

> The Irish labourers will work any time … I consider them very valu-
> able labourers, and we could not do without them. By treating them
> kindly, they will do anything for you … An Englishman could not do
> the work they do. When you push them they have a willingness to
> oblige which the English have not; they would die under anything
> before they would be beat; they would go at hard work till they drop
> before a man should excel them … In his own country he is notori-
> ously lazy and negligent in the extreme; after crossing the channel he
> became a model of laboriousness and enterprise.[57]

Compared to those navvies who built canals and railways in the previ-
ous century, working conditions were allegedly improving during the post-war period. From 1945 onwards, operatives unable to work due to weather conditions were given half pay and workers were guaranteed a thirty-two-hour working week, as well as holidays with pay and extended notice of dismissal.[58] Additionally, in 1948, the working week was reduced from forty-eight to forty-four hours,

and the labour rate, which was 1*s* 4*d* in 1940 had increased to 2*s* 5*d* in 1950.[59] In theory, their lives were improving but in practice there were still a number of loopholes that could make their life as hard as before.

For a start, many labourers were paid cash-in-hand. They did not pay tax, nor did they have a national insurance number. Some of them didn't have a clue what it was, while the others couldn't quite figure out how it worked, or couldn't be bothered to understand the system. Those labourers often used false names or other people's national insurance number. But working 'on the lump' in the long run was risky as they could be entitled to almost nothing – they would get no medical treatment or compensation when they had an accident.

Born in Galway in 1926, Donall MacAmhlaigh left Ireland in 1951 and became one of the navvies. He wrote of his experience of how Irish workers got away with paying taxes:

Plenty of the Irish working over here don't pay income tax at all – they pretend to have a wife and children back home in Ireland. I suppose the tax people find it hard to prove whether that is the case or not, but at all events, they do little enough about it.[60]

While Irish people made more money in England, their standard of living and quality of life did not improve and many of them actually found that their situation had deteriorated. Unfortunately, this was the hard reality for many of those migrant workers. Being a navvy meant that life often revolved around alcohol and Irish people, especially navvies, generally drank more in Britain than they did back home even though a bottle of Guinness cost 1*s* 2*d* in London, compared to 7*d* in Ireland. Quite often, the pub was the only safe haven for Irish people. Because it was impossible for them to stay in their often shared and crowded accommodation, the pub functioned as if it was their living room.

Those migrant workers coming from big families often felt lonely and lost on their own in a big city. While some lucky youngsters found kind landladies who mothered them, others who were not so fortunate began to rely on alcohol as a sole emotional outlet.

In general, women had a better network of family members, church and friends, but their male counterparts tended to suffer from extreme loneliness. In fact, the majority of lonesome youngsters initially started drinking for company. As a result, many developed alcohol-related problems and illnesses after coming to Britain.

Ironically, the pub was also a lifeline for construction workers because it functioned as the place to find jobs, information and get paid. Many navvies were recruited by contractors or sub-contractors and so they often heard about potential job opportunities while having a pint in a pub.

Most of them were uninsured and unregistered, completely outside the legal system; therefore, they believed that they were left without an entitlement to healthcare services or a pension, although this was in fact not the case. Some 'subbies' did not intend to stay in England for too long, so they did not save in case of accident, illness, or for old age, or consider the consequences of their lifestyle and demanding physical work.

They were paid by the lump system – typically paid cash-in-hand by the hour or the day – also in the pub, although this was sometimes very late at night. It has been well documented that many Irish firms carried out abuses of power in collaboration with publicans. A typical scenario involved a cheque, which was handed in to be cashed at 6 p.m., although the money was not handed over until midnight. Navvies would, therefore, drink all night while waiting to get their money. Many priests, like Fr Fullam, acknowledged that there were certainly Irish firms that got rich on the back of exploiting their own. 'The slate' was also a regular trick in many pubs. Another racket was charging the desperate worker ten shillings to cash a cheque so that by the end of the week many unfortunates had very little to draw after wiping the slate clean on a Thursday or Friday.[61]

On top of this, the living conditions that Irish navvies endured were notoriously dreadful. Some Irish people eventually climbed up the ladder, owned large houses and became landlords themselves but unfortunately, they often contributed to these dreadful conditions by giving navvies the same or worse treatment. It became a vicious circle. 'They rented out to their countrymen – sharing by several men with mattresses on the floor, the Irish exploited their own by offering appalling living conditions to those who had no choice but to endure them.'[62]

Another regular problem associated with navvies was fighting. Fights occurred on a regular basis. Donal MacAmhlaigh recalled: 'As I went asleep tonight, the silence was broken with shouting and screaming, dreadful cursing and the noise of heavy blows. It was the Connemara men and the people from Dublin. They've been fighting this many a day.'[63]

Language was another issue. Native Gaelic speakers were often isolated from non-Gaelic speaking Irish people. According to witnesses, Connemara men were often attacked by their fellow Irishmen, just because Gaelic native speakers preferred talking in their own language, and those Irish people became frustrated as they could not understand them.

Apart from being susceptible to vice, another drawback was that many navvies failed to form any proper relationships or friendships throughout their lives, as their work involved moving around from place to place. Sexuality in those days was laden with religious and social taboos and rural Catholics in particular were extremely timid when forming relationships with the opposite sex.

While some navvies had difficulties adjusting to their lives in a new environment, others were discovering new things and opening up new horizons.

Our free day is on Saturday … This is the day of the week I like best and I always spend it the same way. I go to the public baths where I have a good scrub and then I visit the library. An hour or two

goes browsing among the books and I select one or two; then I make
my way round to the market and maybe I have a pint or two in the
Rodney before my dinner.[64]

Peter O'Driscoll from Aughaville, County Cork, had a particularly
inquisitive mind, and his story resonates with many who made up
their minds to do better:

Work was heavy manual labour on construction projects requiring
no special skill. I soon learned that I was spending my wages of
fifteen pounds a week on cigarettes and beer. I was saving less than
I did back in Ireland as a farm labourer in Cork earning three pounds
a week. So I changed my outlook in life from hanging out in pubs,
drinking beer and smoking cigarettes. I quit smoking and started to
work out in a boxing club two evenings a week and jogging in the
parks most evenings after work. I was determined to develop my
physical strength and skills in the art of self-defence. This helped me
to keep my mind off the drinking and smoking. The important lesson
I learned was my pub friends soon resented my new attitude about
life. I was now using my time to read newspapers and magazines
about life in other English cities. I attended movies, Irish dancehalls
and museums which opened my mind to history and life in general.
I learned that life in England was or could be a class society. I thought
Australia was a place of opportunity, until my brother invited me to
emigrate to America.[65]

Being amongst navvies meant that they were constantly under peer
pressure. It was viewed as somewhat unacceptable to be different or
'to get above their station'.
Robert Sheehy, from County Kerry, explains:

I say as it is only all a game of pretending and anyone who doesn't
go along with it will be outcast and outlawed. There is very little
tolerance, if any, for difference in Irish society. Always bear in mind

that the Irish mind set is a very complex one and not everyone
will be comfortable with being told that and very few will actually
tolerate.[66]

Opened in 1905, Arlington House was, and still is, a hostel for
'the poorest of men' on Arlington Road, in Camden Town. Once the
biggest hostel in Europe, it was packed with Irish navvies. In later
years, however, this place became one of the largest residences for
homeless people in Britain and a home to elderly Irishmen, such
as former navvies, who had never dreamed they would remain in
London that long.

In a documentary called *The Men of Arlington* in 2010, Joe
McGarry explained that Arlington House was 'a place where you've
got light, heat and companionship and ultimately all the needs that
a human being needs'. According to the Aisling Return to Ireland
project, which was started by workers in the London Irish Centre
and Arlington House to help vulnerable Irish people, Arlington
House has been home to more Irishmen than any other building
outside Ireland.

Since many navvies had a tough life and suffered from problems
with alcohol, among other things, so when they died – quite often
without any kind of family or recognition – they were buried in
unmarked graves at East Finchley Cemetery in North London.
The oft-quoted adage was that they 'poorly lived, poorly died, poorly
buried and no one cried.'

Many hundreds of men died anonymously at Arlington House.
There is a memorial stone at the cemetery on which Irish poet
Patrick Kavanagh's words from his autobiographical book *The Green
Fool* are etched. It is dedicated to the memory of those men who
were buried anonymously in unmarked graves. The memorial stone
reads: 'Many Irish boys made Rowton (Arlington) House, Camden
Town, first stop from Mayo … The soft voices of Mayo and Galway
sounding in that gaunt impersonal place fell like warm rain on the
arid patches of my imagination.'

Alex McDonnell, the former secretary of the Arlington Irish Association remarked:

> When someone died in Arlington House, and it was a regular occurrence, there would be a brooding sadness in the air. Occasionally someone would cry out 'Last stop Finchley!' with a bit of bravado but without much conviction. A lot of the men were living under assumed names or lying low simply because they felt ashamed that they hadn't fulfilled their youthful ambitions. Sometimes we could get word to a family member and they would find out for the first time that their long-lost father, uncle, son or brother had been living in a hostel. They wouldn't have cared where they ended up but would have preferred to have known them when they were alive.[67]

The Men of Arlington explained that all the Irish navvies wanted was money. Since the money was their top priority, they would come to work, regardless of the conditions.

Considering their naivety and vulnerability, the navvies were more likely to be manipulated and deceived. As a matter of fact, they regularly had to endure exploitation and extreme deprivation. Abusive foremen, especially the ones from Ireland, were commonly found and evidence suggests that many foremen who were in power took advantage of their position and did whatever they wanted to do. Oftentimes, they preferred to hire non-English speakers from Connemara, so that they wouldn't understand the whole situation. That's why it was widely assumed that the Irish were the 'hardest on their own people'.[68]

For instance, a typical Sunday shift worked like this:

> On a Saturday night, a ganger would come into the Half Moon pub on Holloway Road and ask did you want a shift in the morning. If you did, you had to guarantee him a drink the next night … the shift might last from seven o'clock until half past twelve, for about five pounds a shift. No documentation – just a bundle of fivers in the pub, and pay

the men out. Afterwards, when you were driven back to London in the wagons, the foreman came in with you and he had possibly ten shillings off each man, and he drank all day free, and if you didn't go along with that, no more Sunday shifts.[69]

Some gangers were simply cruel and beyond rational: 'Sometimes, a man would be taken out on a job, and the ganger-men took a dislike to him. They'd just dump him in the street and tell him to find your own so-and-so way home.'[70]

Peter O'Driscoll, who worked for construction companies in England echoed the sentiments. The ganger men clearly abused power and bullied their workers:

> Getting you to work past quitting time was the most common one. For example, they would ask you to mix more concrete to finish the job ... The prime duty of a foreman is to get the job done at the least amount of cost or expenses and time is money. I speak for my generation; leaders or foreman are born not trained or educated to lead people. Most foremen that I worked for in England were the largest person on the job and their intent was to dominate you into thinking their way. The rougher and tougher you acted the more they liked it.[71]

Fr Seamus Fullam also acknowledged: 'The Irish ... made the worst foremen. Some of them ... were tyrants. Many of the men I met through the Catholic Club told me they were delighted when they got an Englishman as their foreman.'[72]

Many navvies agreed that English foremen treated Irish navvies with respect.

> I came across a big red-faced man that I knew immediately was a foreman ... I knew from his voice that he was from the West of England. Isn't it strange that he could be so civil to me whereas a man from my own country wouldn't even look at me while he was

addressing me. It's no wonder that Irish foremen have such bad
reputations here when the half of them haven't the manners of a
dog.[73]

One might wonder how the Irish foremen could be so cruel to their
own people. Their authoritarian mindset could be explained by the
fact that while there was a long tradition of labour organisation and
workers' rights in Britain, those mentalities had not yet taken firm
root in Irish minds.[74] Also, the harsh realities of their former life in
Ireland and the depravations suffered might have made them less
empathetic to the suffering of others. It must also be pointed out that
Ireland's history is littered with similar examples of Irish cruelty of
fellow countryman: the Great Famine, for example, was exacerbated
by the actions of some of the Irish landlords.

As early as 1817, a returned emigrant warned that 'on the arrival
of an Irish ship [in America] 'a crowd of poor Irish, who have been
in that country for a number of years, are always fond of meeting
their countrymen on landing, and of encouraging them to take
a share of grog or porter' – and, in effect, to squander the little
capital they had carried overseas. Far more dangerous were the
rapacious porters, lodging-house keepers, ticket brokers for inland
travel, currency exchangers, and employment agents (sometimes
pimps for local brothels) who infested the ports and fleeced the
unwary: 'I have met with so much deception since we have landed
on the shores of the New World,' lamented Francis Rankin, 'that
I am fearful of trusting anyone.'[75]

Brendan O'Sloan, an Irish immigrant in London, observed:

It's partly because life over there in Ireland is hard and poverty has always
been around or close by for many people. The weather and so on can be
very harsh and bleak and I think this sometimes gets into the psychology
of some of the people and they bring out their anger and frustration
on their own. Also Catholicism over the years did not really emphasise
the direct teachings in the bible but sought to control the population

and they did this through fear, fear of God, fear of sinning, even fear of success or achieving, so with a people held down the inbuilt angers were often dispersed at the local level against their own.[76]

Instead of providing better compensation to workers, some construction companies provided them with basic accommodation and food to assure the workers, at a minimal cost of course.

For instance, a well-known 'dirty trick' worked like this:

> We found out today why we get sandwiches every morning on this job. It seems that the contractors get subsistence money from the railway company for every man employed here and instead of paying it over to each man, they arranged for these snacks to be supplied. It's a dirty trick, surely. The two pounds nine would add a tidy bit to the wage-packet but we can't do anything about it. There's no union or any association here to help us stand up for our rights.[77]

A considerable number of people – no one knows how many – were injured and even killed while working. The majority of workers were not aware of any health and safety issues at the time when no one wore protective gear or equipment. John Jones from Kenmare, County Kerry, who briefly worked for a construction company in England, described many people's attitude: 'I didn't give [it] much thought, aside from being careful not to fall off of high buildings.'[78]

Peter O'Driscoll agreed that he was not well informed on safety issues or health risks, either.

> When working for contractors in general, the unions think that by learning a trade you are then aware of the risks associated with your work. The company depends on their first line supervisor on the job to keep the work place safe. A guy like me who was willing to ask questions is not often welcome on the job. Life is 'the accident' that you or I prevent from happening by questioning the supervisor or work place

very few workers appreciate you. But when accidents happen they point fingers. The bottom line is that safety was everyone's business and it is everyone's duty to keep a safe place.[79]

IRISH EMPLOYERS

Many companies benefitted from the outbreak of the Second World War because they provided services before, during and after the conflict by building, repairing and rebuilding. Some of the founders that started their careers as navvies became millionaires by seizing a golden opportunity. Some of the businesses that hired predominantly Irish workers are listed below.

BALFOUR BEATTY
George Balfour, a Scottish mechanical engineer, and Andrew Beatty, an English chartered accountant, formed the company in 1909. From its inception, the company provided services such as general and electrical engineering, railway and lighting properties and contracting in Britain and abroad. One of its major works included developing the London Underground system, for which scores of Irish workers were hired.

CLANCY GROUP
Michael Clancy from County Clare came to work in London in 1948 and formed his own company, M.J. Clancy & Sons Ltd, in 1958. Based in Wembley, north London, this family business contributed to ground, drainage and roadworks in and around London.

COSTAIN
Irish entrepreneur Richard Costain from Colby on the Isle of Man left for England during the Great Famine and started his family business in Liverpool in 1865. Trained as a joiner, he and his future brother-in-law began working as builders and undertakers.

Costain's business gradually but steadily expanded. During the First World War, it built the workforce accommodation for a steel company in Redcar, north-east England. However, it was when the company started building houses in the London suburbs in 1920s that the family business really expanded and it soon took to the global stage. One of the high-profile projects in which Costain was involved was the construction of Dolphin Square in Pimlico, London – the largest block of flats in Europe in those days. Just a year after the construction started in 1935, the first 600 apartments were ready for occupation. Costain had become one of the largest speculative house builders in Britain before the First World War.

During the Second World War, Costain assisted in creating the Mulberry floating concrete harbour that was towed in sections across the English Channel. The company also built airfields and ordnance factories. After the war, Costain constructed countless houses, airports, petrochemical plants, waste treatment works, schools and other infra-structure all across the UK and abroad.

FITZPATRICK & SONS

Pat Fitzpatrick from County Cork came to London to work and later became a street mason. His son, John Martin, also joined his father's profession. It was John who established the civil engineering family company Fitzpatrick & Sons in 1921, specialising in concrete paving. The business also worked on the reconstruction of Parliament Square and repaved the forecourt of Buckingham Palace.

FORD

During the Second World War, the British Government was focused on maintaining commercial and military vehicle production, and the majority of automobile plants were used for aircraft and aero engine production.

As soon as the war ended, passenger car production resumed and the 1950s was a decade of expansion for car industries. The British car industry thrived, providing around 50 per cent of the world's exported vehicles during that decade. Some of the major automobile companies during the 1950s that hugely contributed to the British economy were the British Motor Corporation (BMC); Rootes; Standard-Triumph;Vauxhall and Ford.

Those car factories in Britain heavily relied on Irish workers. For instance, the *Irish Independent* on 16 May 1951 reported that many thousands of people from County Cork were working at Ford in Dagenham, the biggest Ford plant in Europe at that time.

Cork Marina Plant

The founder of the Ford Motor Company was Henry Ford from Michigan, in the US. His father, William, was originally from Ballinascarty, County Cork and emigrated to the US during the Great Famine in 1847. To reconnect to his Irish roots and help the depressed local economy, Henry opened a tractor-manufacturing plant – Henry Ford & Son Ltd – in Cork in 1917, after establishing himself in the US since 1903.

Located on the site of the old Cork Park Racecourse near the marina, the Cork factory was substantial in size, with a floor area of 330,000 sq ft. The factory was the first purpose-built Ford factory outside North America. After the end of the First World War, as the demand for tractors fell sharply from 1921, it began to manufacture components for cars.

Subsequently, there were nearly 2,000 people working at the plant by 1926. As a great number of local people were employed, it functioned as a community, complete with football clubs and various regular events. In 1929, the Cork plant was the sole manufacturer of Ford tractors in the world.

The plant was built and provided many much-needed jobs at what were thought of as good wages. As a consequence, many of the men felt able to marry with the prospects of raising a family.[80]

Ford offered ample opportunities, benefits and hope for local people, but this prosperity did not last long. A severe worldwide economic slump in the 1920s and '30s – the Great Depression – as well as the

Anglo-Irish Trade War had a devastating impact on the Irish industry, and the plant in Cork was no exception. This retaliatory trade war (also called the Economic War) between the Irish Free State and the UK started in 1932 and lasted until 1938. Ford was doing very good business until the British Government imposed import barriers on auto parts and other products that were made in the Irish Free State. As a consequence, the production of tractors at the Cork plant was stopped in 1932. Land and tax exemptions and tariff-free access to the UK market soon forced the American automaker to move its operation base to England.

Dagenham

Ford Dagenham opened in 1931 and at the height of its production in 1951, more than 40,000 workers were employed at the plant. Ford purchased a portion of land at Dagenham Dock from Samuel Williams & Sons Ltd and construction of the Ford factory officially began in 1929, with the plant opening in 1931. Although there was already an assembly plant in Manchester, England, the company decided to open a new plant by the River Thames in Dagenham in 1923 in order to have access to a deep-water port.

The Dagenham site initially operated as a trading estate with Briggs Motor Bodies and Kelsey-Hayes Wheel Company. These two companies worked closely with Ford and were eventually subsumed into Ford Motor Company itself during the 1950s.

Ford transferred production of tractors to the plant in Dagenham, along with its entire Cork workforce. The plant gradually expanded and by 1954, it was estimated that more than 50 per cent of workers in the foundry at Dagenham were from Ireland.

They were known as 'Dagenham Yanks' in Ireland, which was the term applied to the thousands of individuals and families who migrated from Cork to be employed at Ford in England.

A high proportion of Irish residents were found at the Rylands Estate, a housing estate located close to the Ford factory, which was built in the early 1930s. There was also a Catholic church and convent on nearby Goresbrook Road, as well as several Irish social clubs. The area came to be called 'Little Cork', as hundreds of thousands of Corkmen and their family members emigrated to work at Ford in Dagenham for over four decades. Dagenham also earned the nickname the 'Detroit of Europe'.

James O'Sullivan, who went to local St Peter's Catholic Primary School, recalls Dagenham's Little Cork and an Irish population largely comprised of families rather than 'young restless men':

> There were indeed large numbers of Irish in Dagenham at the time, and intriguingly, and in contrast to other Irish areas of greater London, most of the original Dagenham Irish were families, not single men as in Camden and Kilburn areas … Those were the days when women in general stayed at home to raise the family. I cannot recall a single example in my immediate neighbourhood of a woman working outside the home. In my case this was so, except that my dear mother died at age 36 from breast cancer, leaving my father with six children to care for. He coped with this by sending for his sister, my aunt, to come over from Ireland to help care for us – which she did.[81]

Ford Dagenham grew rapidly, with 30,000 workers, mainly Catholics, by 1954. One of the local churches, St Peter's, offered Mass every day, at 6 a.m. and 7 p.m, for approximately 5,000 parishioners.

On the opposite side of Goresbrook Road, there was a popular pub called The Chequers. After finishing work, most of them typically had a quick pint before going to the nearby church. It was a common sight to see a large group of men streaming down Goresbrook Road.

As a young man studying at Jesuit College and University, James O'Sullivan also worked in the evenings at the largest Irish pub in Dagenham, the Anglers Retreat, adjoining the sprawling Ford plant. He remembers that the pub was always overflowing with Irish workers.

The Jesuit Fathers – Robert Nash and Leonard Shell – often talked to Ford workers in the canteen and at the works. The church was always packed with men in particular – approximately two men to every woman. Every seat was filled and quite often, extra chairs had to be used; even then, rows of men stood at the back and down the sides and children sat on the steps at the altar rail.

The missionaries from Ireland were always welcomed wherever they went, such as in the cafés. Many men often invited the priest into their rooms, sat him down on the edge of the bed and told him about their families or showed the photograph of the children or family members back home.

Since there were thousands of them, there was no shortage of entertainment events within the Irish community. At a game between the Thomas McCurtain Hurling and Football Club of St Peter's parish Dagenham and Cork All Ireland champions at the Ford Motor Company sports ground on 12 September 1954, tens of thousands of spectators turned up. Among them were the Bishop Beck of Brentwood, the Irish Ambassador and his wife. The Lord Mayor of Cork, the Mayor of Dagenham and Sir Patrick Hennessy, managing director of the Ford Company, attended a reception dinner for the Cork team the previous day in Dagenham's Civic Centre.

Although the economy in Ireland as a whole was rather grim during the post-war period, quite a few companies hired a considerable number of local people in Cork until things got worse. Apart from Ford, other major enterprises included Dunlops, Sunbeam Wolsey, Irish Steel, Verolme Cork Dockyards, as well as scores of smaller-scaled companies were engaged in the textile, agricultural processing, chemical and printing industries. When those businesses scaled down, local people had no choice but to cross the ocean on the *Innisfallen*, which was the only motor passenger vessel running from Penrose Quay, Cork to Fishguard in South Wales during this time. The ship left Penrose Quay on Mondays, Wednesdays and Fridays and returned from Fishguard on Tuesdays, Thursdays and Saturdays.

With the famous advertising slogan, 'Travel the Inisfallen Way', it also
carried livestock and general cargo.

M.J. GLEESON

Michael Joseph Gleeson and his brother emigrated to England from
their small farm in Cloonmore, County Galway, in around 1900, in
search of work. Michael, often called MJ, was more determined and
ambitious, while his brother struggled with homesickness and shortly
after returned to Galway. MJ then moved to Sheffield and worked as a
bricklayer for an Irish builder who was also from Cloonmore. In 1903,
MJ took control of the building firm after marrying its owner's daughter. He changed the company name to M.J. Gleeson in 1915.

MJ established himself in the construction business in Sheffield,
but the ardent businessman was looking for more opportunities to
expand. In the 1920s, his building operations developed beyond
Sheffield to such locations as Manchester, Fleetwood, Preston and
London. During this decade, he also acquired a greyhound stadium
and several local cinemas. MJ was solidly expanding his business and
during the Second World War, his company constructed aerodromes,
airfields, military camps and hospitals all over Britain, under the
instruction of the British Government.

In the 1950s, knowing that a housing shortage was a serious problem,
forward-thinking Gleeson focused on the housing and property development market in London. A countless number of countrymen were
hired to work for MJ's thriving construction empire.

LAING

Along with his family members, James Laing officially began his trade
by building houses in Cumberland in 1848. As his family business
expanded, his grandson John decided to make it a limited company
in London in 1920. In the 1950s, the company hired approximately
10,000 workers for all kinds of reconstruction projects. The majority
were from Ireland, and they worked on the lump.

LOWERY

Peteen Lowery from Cornamona, County Galway, established his own company in London in 1950 after working as a navvy in London. A great number of Galway men were hired by his company, which had 'plenty of lorries'. A generous man, Lowery apparently looked after his county people well. One of them was Donal MacAmhlaigh, who knew Peteen very well and was happy to work for him. He remarked: 'It's wonderful how Lowery got on since he came here. He was only a navvy like the rest of us until he started up on his own and now he has a contracting business almost as big as Murphy over there in Finsbury Park.'[82]

SIR ROBERT MCALPINE & SONS

One of the most well-known construction companies that is strongly associated with Irish navvies is McAlpine. Sir Robert McAlpine, also known as 'Concrete Bob', established this civil engineering firm in 1869. McAlpine, a Scotsman, began his career at the bottom of the ladder, as a bricklayer and builder who could lay a minimum of approximately 2,000 bricks per day. From his own experience, he once said: 'The Scots made the best gangers, the Irish the best labourers and the English the best customers'.

McAlpine became famous for hiring scores of Irish workers because of their loyalty to the company. There is an anecdote behind his Irish preference, however. When the company was in financial trouble in the 1920s, McAlpine asked his workers to stick with him without pay for a couple of months, with the promise of reward when he turned his business around. Many local men who needed to support their families left, but the Irish workers who had nowhere to go had no choice but to stay with the company.

McAlpine eventually became a fast-growing firm and there was always plenty of work for Irish people. There is a veritable account on how McAlpine was responsible for countless major construction projects over several decades, and Irish workers were a constant part of the process. According to the joke, a teacher asks: 'Who made the

Irish workmen, or McAlpine's Fusiliers, laying the foundations for a new
block of flats in Kilburn Square, Willesden.

world?' And a child responds: 'McAlpine, Sir – and my Daddy laid
the bricks.'

Due to their ubiquitous presence in the building trade, another
quip goes as follows: 'McAlpine went by motor car. And Wimpey
went by train. But Paddy tramped the Great North Road, and got
there just the same.'

Although McAlpine was firmly established in business before
the war, during the post-war construction boom, it contributed
extensively to the economy as there was plenty of work to be done.

McAlpine was heavily involved in building countless office blocks and commercial buildings and repairing bombed-out streets to keep the traffic moving.

For instance, one of the most remarkable buildings they constructed was the Shell Centre on the South Bank, which stands at 107m (351ft) with twenty-seven stories, plus three stories below ground. This was the first London office tower, exceeding the height of the Victoria Tower of the Palace of Westminster. Completed in 1961, McAlpine and his Irish workers were the major labour force on this project. The work was physically intensive, particularly 'in the pile-boring and in the excavation of the huge basins to take thousands of tons of liquid cement which form the concrete foundations of the building.'[83]

Apart from this major building, McAlpine also took part in various other projects on the South Bank, which was being extensively developed during the 1950s. Hundreds of thousands of Irish people were working on those building sites and living in the vicinity of the South Bank and around Elephant and Castle, which was at that time known as a slum district. McAlpine was not just a profit-centred domineering firm but it had invested in sizable philanthropic activities. Knowing that more than 80 per cent of the McAlpine's workers were Irish and almost all of them were Catholics, the company built many Mass centres and churches all across the country.

When interviewed by a newspaper reporter, Fr Denis Walshe responded:

I found Sir Robert McAlpine most helpful in providing facilities for the many thousands of Irish they employed during those war years to attend Mass and the sacraments … and at that period the Irish workers in most cases lived in the camps on the building sites.[84]

The company would not have survived and thrived without Irish labourers. As Robert McAlpine lay dying, he is reputed to have said that should his workforce wish to mark his passing, they might be allowed two minutes' silence, but that they should keep the big mixer going and keep Paddy behind it.

MCNICHOLAS

Mayoman Pat McNicholas initially came to work in England as a navvy but ended up establishing his own company in 1949. With his brother, Michael 'Pincher' McNicholas, he specialised in digging holes for cables and pipes, and the company contributed greatly to the telecommunications, gas and water industries during the post-war reconstruction period, hiring many Mayomen.

MOWLEM

A stonemason from Dorset named John Mowlem established his own company in 1822. The firm gradually expanded and by the 1950s, it became one of the largest construction and civil engineering firms in Britain. Relying on the Irish labour force, Mowlem was engaged in reconstruction work of bomb-damaged buildings.

J. MURPHY & SONS

John James Murphy was born in Loughmark, near Cahersiveen, County Kerry, in 1913. He attended the local school in Curickeens, left school at the age of 15 and travelled to London in search of a job in the late 1930s. Like everybody else at that time, he worked for an array of construction companies but he eventually started up as a subcontractor in the building trade.

The Second World War offered him a glorious opportunity; his nascent business started picking up smoothly by getting involved with variety of war-related construction projects such as building new airfields. By the end of the war, he was a well-established businessman in England. Based in Kentish Town, north London, his other businesses included electrification, cable installation, water facilities and road building. Murphy was partial to his countrymen and countless Irishmen – mostly Kerrymen – were hired over the decades.

A modest, hardworking, adaptable and driven businessman, he was a member of the Irish Club at Eaton Square and occasionally visited the club.

His brother Joseph followed in his footsteps and they worked together for ten years. After they went separate ways, John's men worked at ground level or above, while Joe's workers mainly worked underground. They were called 'the Green and the Grey' because John used green vans, while Joe's workers drove grey cars.

Like many construction companies in the 1950s, Murphy used the lump system. This is how Murphy's men were treated:

> In this era of little regulation, the labour the Murphys took on was 'on the lump', that is, hired directly off the street. In the wider construction industry of that time, it was common for there to be a verbal agreement about pay, often by the hour and in cash, with nothing being signed. True identities were not divulged, so 'Eamonn Andrews' could be working on a hundred different sites in one day. With the anonymity came no tax or national insurance deductions. But also came no responsibility if a man was injured; when one died, his name was sometimes unknown. It was a brutal system.[85]

From his humble beginnings, Murphy became one of Britain's wealthiest people by the time he died at the age of 95 in 2009. He was known as a modest but fiercely ambitious man.

At his funeral, the congregation was told how an engineer, under pressure from 'the boss' to complete a job, observed that 'Rome wasn't built in a day'. The boss replied: 'Murphy wasn't around then.'[86]

After nearly eighty years building up the construction empire in England, he was laid to rest in his native County Kerry.

TARMAC
The company was founded by Edgar Purnell Hooley in 1903, after he patented the road-surfacing material tarmac. The business operates

as a road construction and maintenance subcontractor, as well as producing road-surfacing materials. Like many other major construction companies, Tarmac expanded rapidly during and after the Second World War by surfacing large numbers of airfields. Irish workers were the valuable part of this work.

By 1953, Hooley's business was one of the major precast concrete undertakings in Britain, processing more than 2 million tons of slag a year. By 1960, Tarmac's road surfacing had developed into a major civil engineering business within Britain and become a major national road stone and contracting company.

WATES GROUP

Edward Wates and his three brothers established this company in 1897. During the 1920s and '30s, Edward's son, Norman, Sir Ronald and Allan, expanded their family business by pioneering speculative house building and then extended their activities into general contracting. Like other construction firms, Wates built aerodromes, factories and army camps during the Second World War, and diversified into constructing pre-cast and *in situ* reinforced concrete barges and floating docks. It also supplied major parts of the Mulberry harbours that were towed across the English Channel after D-Day.

Wates Group built more than 60,000 houses and flats during the reconstruction period, by using the high-rise and low-rise industrialised housing system developed by the company. In addition to the core housing, contracting and plant businesses, property development was added to the portfolio in the 1950s.

Apart from the above-mentioned companies, many more Irish construction businesses existed on a smaller scale all through Britain.

GEORGE WIMPEY

This construction and house-building company was established in Hammersmith in 1880. Due to the substantial number of Irish workers they hired, it was said that Wimpey stood for 'We Import More Paddies Every Year'.

In the immediate post-war period, building controls prevented any substantial return to private-house building but by the early 1950s, Wimpey was building around 18,000 local authority houses a year in Britain and soon became the country's most prolific house builder. In the 1950s, Wimpey was also steadily expanding its building and civil engineering portfolios both domestically and abroad, and it quickly became one of the larger international construction companies.

TAYLOR WOODROW

Frank Taylor founded this construction and house-building company with his uncle Jack Woodrow in 1921. It had become a high-profile construction company by the end of the war. As Frank Taylor urgently needed workers for his company, he sent an Irish agent to County Mayo on a recruitment drive in 1942. Within just two months, 1,000 men, accompanied by a priest, arrived in Liverpool. They worked backbreaking ten-hour shifts and overtime every day. Their rate was 3s 6d.

By the 1950s, the company was successfully expanding both domestically and internationally. In Britain, Taylor Woodrow was the contractor for London Heathrow airport; the Liverpool Metropolitan Cathedral; and Calder Hall, the world's first commercial nuclear power station, amongst other things. In London, it was heavily involved with private-house building, especially once building controls were abolished.

PUBLIC SERVICES

LONDON TRANSPORT

Another sector populated by predominantly Irish workers was London Transport, or LT. LT was originally created in 1933 from bus, tram, trolleybus and Tube operators run by both private companies and municipal authorities.

LT struggled to hire local people who were unwilling to do 'lousy jobs'. According to a LT brochure, it openly admitted this by saying: 'It became especially hard to fill the lower grade, poorly paid jobs that could be dirty and difficult, involving shift work and long hours.'

Although Irish people had been synonymous with LT ever since its inception, LT began to actively recruit workers from Ireland by setting up recruitment offices in Dublin, Belfast and other loca-tions in the 1950s. The Ministry of Labour placed advertisements in local newspapers and job announcements were broadcast on the radio. LT recruited both men and women between twenty and thirty-five years old to work as bus drivers, bus conductors, railway workers, station men and women and canteen workers, among other positions.

London's tram system was closed in 1952 due to wartime damage. As a consequence, the design of a new bus, called the Routemaster or the RM-type – based on aircraft technology, using aluminium panels for the body construction – was introduced in 1956 and quickly began operating on London streets.

John Lydon from County Galway worked for LT for thirty years. The job could be unpleasant at times, as people did not show proper respect towards bus drivers.

> I arrived in Euston after getting the train from Crewe. To get to know my way around London, I followed the number 24 bus which went from Hampstead Heath to Pimlico … I began cleaning bus chassis at the age of 36 at Hanwell garage. The chassis had to be a bright silver colour before they could be tested. In order to reach the underneath, we'd use a device called a table-tilter which tilted the bus sideways. I washed about six a day on my own and cleaned coaches, too. When we were cleaning, if ever we had drunk people who had stayed on to the depot we'd hose them down to get them off the buses. Some of the coaches were in a terrible mess inside. But it could be a profitable business cleaning the coaches especially as you often got tips from

the coach companies. You got very used to the buses when you were cleaning I could even tell which bus driver had been driving from the position of the seat. After this, I drove number 18 buses from Wembley to Euston. I was a driver for six years until I had a heart attack and couldn't carry on. To begin with I hadn't been able to drive buses because of my height but I learnt while I was cleaning and then they agreed to let me drive. I can remember driving up to twelve buses a day. It was difficult being a driver as you didn't get much respect from the passengers. There was no screen and some-times people spat.[87]

Despite their not-so-well-paid work − which included working often long and unsocial hours − most Irish migrant workers appeared to be extremely satisfied with their new jobs, according to *London Transport Magazine* in the 1950s. Almost all surnames mentioned in the magazine are Irish: Fitzgerald, Gallagher, Walsh, Lynch, Quinn, Doyle, Murphy, O'Connor, McKitterick, O'Leary, O'Shea, Kerr and Fitzsimmons, to name a few. LT is known to have looked after their staff well and organised various social events and sports clubs such as cricket, hockey, football and horse riding for both male and female staff. Most articles in the magazine are about those fun activities, and each picture is accompanied by a caption that most certainly includes Irish surnames and their smiling faces, typically beaming from ear to ear.

The 1950s were the peak time for LT clubs and societies. Popular clubs included a bowling association; the LT Players for music and dramatic societies, which performed in the West End; a rifle club; a canine club; a horticultural society; a flying club, and a Junior Staff Club for LT employees aged under 21.

There was a featured article in the company magazine headlined 'The Irish Come to Town' in October 1951, explaining how Irish people were enjoying their new lives at LT. Due to the shortage of housing in Britain, the company, under the auspices of the welfare department, provided a hostel for newcomers, with a huge recreation room equipped with billiards, table tennis, darts and chess. Mrs Taylor, a matron of the hostel, apparently looked after young lodgers well by washing and ironing their shirts, as well as hosting birthday parties. According to the article, nearly everyone was Irish at the hostel and they enjoyed swimming, dancing, playing sports, and going to the city centre of London to see various shows and entertainment.

By 1956, LT had 87,000 workers. It is believed that there was no discrimination in LT at that time. The majority of employees were immigrants. From the mid-1950s onwards, a large influx of Commonwealth immigrants, from the West Indies in particular, joined the company and foreign bus drivers, tube workers and general LT workers became a common sight. These joined the Irish workers from both the Republic of Ireland and Northern Ireland. As these groups shared rural backgrounds and the struggle to adapt to their new environment, they worked and integrated well together and apparently formed a sense of comradeship.

The benefits of a multicultural society were immense, as the newly arrived Irish immigrants developed tolerance for one another and learned to balance themselves well in two worlds. They worked and bonded well with equally numerous newcomers from the Commonwealth countries.

POLICE

Ever since the Metropolitan Police was established in 1829, Irish police officers have been seen in every department. Working in the police force meant security and respect.

Constant advertisements for 'job opportunities for men in the police force in England' in Irish newspapers throughout the post-war years were highly successful in attracting Irish youngsters. One of the advertisements ran as follows:

Looking for a good job? Starting pay will be £7.6s a week, regular increases, generous allowances and holidays and a pension when you are still young enough to enjoy it. This is what Police Force offers. Keen men between the ages of 19-30, min height 5'9" (5'8" for ex-servicemen). Send at once while there are still thousands of vacancies for a free copy of 'Opportunities in the Police Force in England', which tells you how to prepare rapidly in your home for the entrance test under 'no pass, no fee' terms. Write now and the handbook will be sent free.

B.T.I., 782 Avon House, 356 Oxford St., London W1.[88]

Some aggressive initiatives were necessary, as there was an urgent need for a public order during the 1950s when London was subject to all kinds of demonstrations and protests, as well as an increasing crime rate. Regular articles can be found in the newspapers on police clashing with violent protesters during this period.

As there were many Catholics in the police force, an association called the Catholic Police Guild – or CPG – of England and Wales was founded in 1914, with approval of the Roman Catholic Archdiocese of Westminster. Established in response to representations made by Catholic people serving in the Metropolitan and City of London Police Forces, CPG functioned as a fraternal organisation in order to cater to the spiritual needs of Roman Catholic service people. Although it has no records of members' origin, Brendan McWilliams from CPG acknowledged that many of their members would have come from Ireland.

Police forces were dominated by men, and there was still only a handful of female officers in the 1950s. The Metropolitan Police's Women Police Service was set up in 1914 by Margaret Damer Dawson, an anti-white slavery campaigner, and Nina Boyle, a militant suffragette journalist. The initial aims were to have a uniformed organisation to deter pimps and discourage young girls and women from entering prostitution, and to allow women to take on roles during the war previously held by men.

Female officers' beats tended to be the red-light districts such as brothels, nightclubs and betting houses as well as railway terminals, recruiting stations and parks, where newly arrived girls and women from Ireland would congregate. In those days, female police officers were expected just to observe and focus on gathering evidence; they were to call in male police officers when a crime was being committed. They were not allowed to carry handcuffs. From 1923, they were finally given limited power of arrest and in 1930, A4 Branch, or Women Police, was launched under a female superintendent. Since Women's Special was introduced in 1950, female officers took on increased responsibility and became a more noticeable presence on London streets.

THE NHS

The Welfare State was introduced by Clement Attlee's labour government in 1945 and the National Health Service was established three years later with the aim of providing free healthcare for all – rich and poor. The lives of working-class people in Britain were improving considerably, but the advent of the NHS meant that more nurses were urgently required.

As hospitals were having difficulties recruiting enough local nurses, it was forced to start a huge recruitment campaign elsewhere, and so government agencies aggressively recruited Irishwomen in Ireland. Compared to domestic workers, the nursing and teaching professions were regarded as more popular, attractive and respectable, due to better promotion prospects in the long term.

In reality, it was more difficult to be a teacher than a nurse; becoming a teacher meant going to university to get a degree, but unfortunately most parents could not afford the university fees for their children. On the other hand, NHS hospitals provided education and training, which led to a decent lifelong and satisfying profession. Furthermore, many promotion opportunities and incentives for the future existed. However, it was a physically demanding profession with many rigid rules and regulations; it was sometimes said that 'working as a nurse was like being in the army'.[89]

The discipline imposed by matron was typically harsh and the training was intensive, but it was a secure job and student nurses were provided with nurse houses and other benefits. Many Irish women naturally took the nursing route when they had a chance, because 'the training was free and the regime in England wasn't nearly as harsh as in Ireland'.[90]

Always accompanied by visually appealing photos, countless advertisements and articles on nurse recruitment appeared in newspapers after the creation of the NHS. For instance, one advertisement read as follows:

Here's Another Happy Girl – What About You?
We need the help of girls of 17½ years and over who look upon nursing as a worthwhile job. To the girl who is interested in becoming a nurse, we offer a career full of happiness with ample opportunity for advancement. Girls of character and good educational standard will find that nursing is a vocation which opens the doors to interesting work far beyond the normal environments of hospital routine. The hospital is within easy reach of the centre of London. Training allowance first year £200, second year £210, third year £225, less £100 pa, for board and lodging.

The article was accompanied by a photo of an attractive nurse in a crisp white uniform with the caption: 'Please write a letter to me – I will be happy to send you full particulars. The Matron, Wanstead hospital, London E11'[91]

Another incentive for young women from Ireland was that NHS hospitals awarded medals for Irish girls and also chose poster girls. Newspaper articles typically covered positive, happily smiling and successful Irish immigrant stories. When a girl was selected, as was often the case, the ceremonial event was typically written in an article for the public to read which functioned as an irresistible advertisement. A typical 'article' ran as follows:

Irish Nurse's New Role
From the posters on the hoardings, which seek to recruit nurses, a new face will soon smile down on the passers-by. It is that of a Roscommon

girl, Miss Kitty Fitzmaurice, who has been for the last year pursuing her profession in a Tooting hospital. She is dark and slender with a broad smile which wins everybody by its warm-heartedness. Sometime ago she was chosen by those who work with her as their ideal nurse. Most days she wears little or no make-up and with her clear complexion and dark hair, has no need of it…She has two elder sisters who trained in the same hospital, and that has helped her a good deal. Twice a year, if they can, the girls go back to their farm-home in Cannacht [*sic*]. Other nurses say that they are glad an Irish girl was chosen because so many nurses on all the staffs have what their Scottish and English sisters call 'brogues'.[92]

Nursing was closely connected to religious orders in Ireland. Many typical recruits – most of whom were still just teenagers – were from rural areas with Leaving Certificate honours or a pass from Catholic-administered secondary schools. For many of them, nursing was their first and only career choice and they made multiple applications to hospitals in an effort to secure a place in nurse training.

Founded in 1916, the Royal College of Nursing, or RCN, is an organisation for nurses, midwives, healthcare support workers and nursing students. Although many people from Ireland joined NHS hospitals, nursing shortages remained severe in Britain during the 1950s as demand surpassed supply and working conditions remained rather inadequate.

As nursing was such a popular profession for young women in Ireland, many Irish hospitals typically had waiting lists for a nursing training position. The majority of Irishwomen chose to be trained in NHS hospitals in England because of the massive and relatively organised recruitment process. The Preliminary Training School lasted for three months. The elimination criteria from nursing was failing two of the weekly exams in succession; having an affair with a member of the staff; smoking in uniform; and allowing one of the patients in your care to get a bedsore. Nevertheless, future nurses went through strenuous training amid facing new challenges.

A group of workers at St Joseph's Hospice in Hackney, 1955.

The first morning in class was a shock. We were already rigged out
in white starched uniforms and caps, and given the books we had
to study from, for which we had to pay. The principle tutor stood
beside a hanging skeleton, and in front of a table with a box of bones,
which rattled when moved onto a desk. Then after being addressed as
nurses she marched us all off to the hospital chapel where we prayed
for God's blessing in our work and sang 'All creatures great and small'.
This was more than a surprise to me as my parish priest referred to
England in terms of being pagan. Lectures were in the morning after
prayers, and practical work in the afternoons. There was very little
time for homesickness, as we were driven as though there was no
tomorrow. The majority of the staff were Irish, including the matron,
and assistant matron. The working week was forty-eight hours, no pay
for overtime or time off in lieu. The pay was three pounds a month,
with full board and free training. With the pay packet came a coupon
for a slice of bacon and an egg. This was very welcome as food was
rationed, the stable diet being mostly potatoes, bread and custard …
I qualified in three years and Mrs Clement Atlee, the Prime Minister's
wife, presented the certificates.[93]

Irish nurses seem to have found promotion easier and faster than
other immigrant nurses. Although there were many West Indian
nurses at NHS hospitals who were also recruited from their home
country, Irishwomen were able to take up opportunities not
readily available to black women at this time, such as SRN (State
Registered Nurse) training. This training was seen as higher status
and had better promotion prospects than that for SENs (State
Enrolled Nurses).

Hundreds of thousands of Irish nurses were working in NHS hospitals
all over the country in the 1950s. In London alone, Irish nurses could be
found in St Joseph's Hospice in Hackney, University College Hospital
in Camden, St Andrew's Hospital in Neasden, St James's Hospital in
Balham, Whipps Cross Hospital in Leytonstone, Whittington Hospital
in Archway, St Thomas's Hospital in Lambeth, King's College Hospital

in Southwark, The Royal Waterloo Hospital for Children and Women in Waterloo, General Lying-In Hospital in Lambeth, South Western Hospital in Stockwell, Lambeth Hospital, Kennington, Annie McCall Maternity Hospital in Stockwell and South London Hospital for Women in Clapham.

Moreover, a continuous flow of Irish nurses and other medical professions were also arriving to be employed in non-NHS hospitals and Catholic nursing homes such as Nazareth House in Hammersmith. For instance, a non-NHS hospital, the Catholic Nursing Institute on Lambeth Road, was run by the sisters of Our Lady of Consolation and employed principally Irish nurses.

Many hundreds of Irish nurses were trained at the hospital of St John & St Elizabeth under the supervision of the Sisters of Mercy. It was one of the largest and last remaining hospitals in London not run by the NHS. In order to support the hospital financially – with the help of the St Marylebone Council of the Knights of St Columbia – it held an annual ball, which was one of the highlights of Catholic social life in London. An annual event held in November invited many Irish artists and over 1,000 guests. The event held on 20 November 1950 raised more than £436 – a copious amount of money in those days.

LONDON FIRE BRIGADE

Just before the Second World War broke out, the Auxiliary Fire Service, or AFS, a voluntary fire service to supplement the regular fire brigade, was formed. At that time, the London Fire Brigade had 2,500 officers and foremen, and the AFS needed to recruit and train 28,000 firemen. Because most young men had joined the army, the AFS was forced to rely on those people who were too old or young for the army. Women were also accepted into the brigade for the first time.

During the air raids on London, firemen were extremely busy dealing with explosions on top of their regular work of putting out fires. The most dangerous call-outs involved bombs falling on

Two nurses dancing at a benefit event for the hospital of St John and St Elizabeth.

warehouses where products such as highly flammable alcohol and paint were stored.

During the Second World War, women typically worked as fire watchers and drivers, managed the communications network and worked in mobile canteen vans, but did not fight fires. When the war ended, the majority of women were discharged from the fire service and only a few women remained in the National Fire Service.

Due to the high number of Catholic servicemen, the Catholic Fire Service Guild was established in the end of 1949 in London. With the blessing of Cardinal Griffin, it held its first annual meeting in January 1950 and eventually the movement spread the guild to other British cities.

In September 1950, requiem Mass was offered at St Joseph's church in Wembley for all members of the fire services who lost their lives in the war. A large number of uniformed members of the Catholic Fire Service Guild were present to pay respect.

THE GENERAL POST OFFICE

The General Post Office, or GPO, was another workplace in which Irish people were dominant. By 1959, more than 360,000 were employed by the GPO, which was a government department. The British Postal Museum and Archive does not have records that indicate where GPO employees were coming from, particularly in this time period but it is clear from the documents in the archives that constant recruitment activities were organised on Irish soil throughout the post-war period.

Amongst a substantial proportion of West Indian or Commonwealth immigrant workers, so-called 'aliens' such as Germans, Italians, Hungarians and Polish were hired, along with overwhelming numbers of Irish workers. But people from Ireland were seemingly treated differently from other foreigners, as a note in the archive documents in 1949 states: 'Employment of aliens: Citizens of Eire. Undertaking given by Prime Minister that such citizens will not be treated as foreigners for purposes of Crown Employment.' Although this phrase is somewhat ambiguous, Irish people were apparently not treated like continental Europeans. There is a dedicated file referred to as the 'schedule of employees of Irish origin working on the Up Special TPO [Travelling Post Office]', on which letters were sorted on the journey between London Euston and Glasgow. It was compiled following the Great Train Robbery, which involved the hijack of the London-bound train and the theft of millions of pounds, of 1963. It was one of the most notorious robberies in British criminal history. The robbery was an inside job and a couple of robbers were noted as having Irish accents.

THE BRITISH ARMY

Throughout the course of history, Irish people have been fighting, for various reasons, for or against the English or British in all corners of the world. The Irish military diaspora has been widely recognised, as it has been a long tradition. The Victorian historian Thomas Babington Macaulay once called Ireland 'an inexhaustible nursery of the finest soldiers'.

The economic downturn in Ireland and limited recruitment by the Irish Army always increased the number of Irish recruits joining the British Army and other foreign forces. They risked their lives in order to receive material compensation, to gain specific skills and remuneration, as was the custom. From an immigrant's point of view, it was often said, 'three meals a day, free clothes and excitement are a big draw when times are hard at home. Hard times are the norm.'[94]

In the thirteenth century, English kings recruited many Irishmen in Ireland in order to fight for England in Wales. Even around 600 years later, in 1832, Irishmen comprised nearly 50 per cent of the non-commissioned ranks of the British Army. Furthermore, countless Anglo and Protestant Irishmen served as officers. As a consequence, almost a quarter of army officers were Irish by 1871.

Until the late eighteenth century, Irish Catholics were not allowed to join the military and political office in Ireland, so the tradition of joining the foreign army was established. Irish soldiers who joined continental European armies between the sixteenth and eighteenth centuries were called the Wild Geese. They served for the Spanish, French, Austrian, Italian, Swedish and Polish armies – until it was declared illegal to join continental European armies in 1745.

During the American Civil War, more than 150,000 Irishmen fought for the union side and 25,000 for the confederate side. Needless to say, many lost their lives on both sides of the war.

Irishmen made great soldiers, as they were resilient and tough souls who could handle the cold, dull foods and other austere conditions. According to Diego Brochero de Anaya, who wrote to the Spanish king, Philip III, in 1598 about the lack of sailors in the Armada:

> … every year Your Highness should order to recruit in Ireland some Irish soldiers, who are people tough and strong, and nor the cold weather or bad food could kill them easily as they would with the Spanish, as in their island, which is much colder than this one, they are almost naked, they sleep on the floor and eat oats bread, meat and water, without drinking any wine.[95]

Wherever there is a war, there are fighting Irishmen. An article from the *Catholic Herald* suggested that their popularity as a fighting force was due to 'the Irishman's love of a fight, his breathless audacity and exuberant disregard of personal danger'. Their laudable reputation as great soldiers enhanced military recruitment in Britain and beyond.

For a long time, there has been a continuous influx of Irish people serving for numerous Irish regiments in the British Army. One of the most discernible regiments is the Irish Guards. Established in 1900 by Queen Victoria, the Irish Guards was created to commemorate the bravery of the Irish people who fought in the Second Boer War for the British Empire. The first recruit was called James O'Brien from Limerick, and many Irish people followed as a free transfer and other benefits were offered. The Irish Guards played a leading part in both the First and Second World Wars. They won a total of six Victoria Crosses, which include the last one to be presented in the Second World War.

Dozens of events for the fighting Irish were held in the post-war years. After a couple of men from Ireland won the Victoria Cross, a parade was organised in Hyde Park in June 1956. During this ceremony, Major Edward 'Micky' Mannock said:

> What do you think of the average Irishman as a pure fighter – compared with any other European and why? Well, Mick, the average Irishman, with his mixture of Celtic and Norman blood, is not only a gifted but a natural fighter. Blood is blood and breed is breed and ever the twain will tell.[96]

The Irish Guards was originally nicknamed Bob's Own after the first colonel of the Regiment, Lord Roberts, but they are now affectionately known as the Micks or Fighting Micks. The term Micks could be a derogatory term depending on the context, but it is considered praiseworthy within the army.

According to *Irish Guards Association Journal*, recruitment figures for 1958 were not as good as the previous year, but this fall was common to the whole army. This was due to the British Government's decision to end National Service, and the announcement of proposed cuts to the army. Nevertheless, the publication noted that their recruiting figures were still much better than most regiments in the army. This was the first regiment to stop taking national servicemen, and by 1959, the regiment would be almost entirely composed of regular soldiers. Approximately 70 per cent of the recruits in 1958 were Irish born – a further increase from the previous years.

The Women's Royal Army began to recruit women in a non-nursing capacity for the first time in 1917. After the Women's Army Auxiliary Corps (later named Queen Mary's Army Auxiliary Corps) was formed in the same year, the number of women joining the army gradually increased.

According to *Soldier*, the British Army magazine, the Queen Alexandra's Royal Army Nursing Corps – the nursing branch of the British Army – initiated an aggressive recruitment drive of women from 1950s onwards. They were hired to work as radiographers, masseuses, clinical workers and special treatment orderlies among other roles. Many women with Irish surnames were featured in articles all through the 1950s. The magazine also noted that the number of female recruits from overseas was lower than during the Second World War, but 'Irish women were always present in the Army'.[97]

Soldier explained that there were three reasons why girls wanted to join the army. Firstly, they needed companionship. London was a big city but could be the loneliest place in the world; they would like to be in a group and share their lives with others. Secondly, many girls wanted security. Receiving a regular salary was always attractive and the army job gave them a sense of security. And lastly, the spirit of adventure was clearly the big factor for youngsters. The magazine survey showed that almost all recruits wanted to go overseas.

A typical advertisement advised potential applicants that they must be between seventeen-and-a-half and thirty-six years old, must supply two references, pass the medical test and be prepared to serve anywhere. They were allowed to buy themselves out, however. The cost during the first three months was £15; £5 less than the charge for men.

DOMESTIC WORKERS

Compared to Ireland, Britain offered diverse job opportunities specifically for women. In the 1950s, the low average rates of unemployment, approximately 3 per cent, did not include the majority of women who were considered economically inactive in Britain.

Domestic service, which included house cleaning, cooking, gardening, childcare and personal services was the top occupation for Irish girls and women in Britain. In fact, domestic service was the second largest category of employment in England during the Victorian era, after agricultural work. The contribution of countless Irish domestic servants was not just enormous but meritorious.

At the outbreak of the Second World War, approximately 2 million women were employed in domestic service, and their wages were 25*d* a week. Although the number of domestic workers had visibly decreased by the 1950s in England as more Irishwomen went into nursing, factory and clerical work, it was still the most popular and easiest profession to get into in order to leave Ireland as it didn't require any qualifications.

Irishwomen were commonly seen in affluent areas of the city, where they also resided. In 1951, there were more Irishwomen than men in England. In Kensington, in particular, Irishwomen exceeded Irishmen by as much as 3:1 owning to the number of domestic workers in private houses and hotels. They could also be found working as chambermaids at prestigious hotels such as the Savoy Hotel in the Strand and in the catering business.

There were some obvious reasons for choosing to be a domestic worker as it was historically and traditionally Irish women's primary profession within the British system. This way of thinking was not unique to Britain; hundreds of thousands of Irish domestic workers also went to the US, Canada, Australia, New Zealand and other countries.

Unlike the many domestic servants hired in relatively wealthy households in the US (called 'Bridgets') who were clearly visible and recognised in American cities, their British counterparts remained inconspicuous, despite their equally large numbers and stupendous contribution to the economy. Still, the treatment they received in

Britain was considered much more humane than in Ireland. As a matter of fact, Irish domestic workers were treated relatively well by their employers in Britain, and even better in the US, whereas they were treated as second-class citizens and inferiors back home. They also received higher wages in Britain and the employment package often included accommodation, food and other rewards. Also, the job was much less demanding in London compared to working in rural areas in Ireland, which could be physically and psychologically much harder.

Domestic service has often been considered as the ultimate women's work. The Commission on Youth Unemployment of 1951 even encouraged Irish women to get into the profession by claiming that domestic service helped to train girls and women for their natural vocation – the care and management of home and children.

One of the unique features of this trade is that would-be domestic workers left Ireland relatively young. For example, of every 100 girls in Connacht aged between 15 and 19 in 1946, 42 had left by 1951.[98] As many of them were barely teenagers, various politicians and clergy planned to stop this trend. Among these outspoken politicians was Seán MacBride, who was strongly against the emigration of women under the age of 21. Fine Gael's James Dillon also wished to impose restrictions somehow, but others believed that there was nothing to be done to dissuade those who wanted to leave.

Fr Jeremiah Newman, Professor of Sociology and Catholic Action at Maynooth, suggested the government should investigate the possibility of emigration restrictions of the girls under the age of 18 but it would have been impossible to ban them from emigrating as their reasons for leaving could not be proven. For instance, they could be simply going to receive an education overseas or had been adopted by relatives in foreign countries.

Some of our emigrants are unsuitable candidates for emigration. Those very young people – and they are many – who leave before they have adequately investigated the possibility of finding work at home are often acting against their own better interests, something of which they are unaware, through immaturity until it is too late … Ireland should certainly do something in regard to the financing of the Irish Centre in Britain. All we ask for is that some financial help should be given to existing Irish reception centres and to such further ones as maybe set up by voluntary initiative in the future.[99]

WEST END THEATRE

Along with other entertainment facilities, the theatre in London flourished in the 1950s. Amongst scores of Irish workers working at theatres, the first female manager at the West End Theatre was an Irishwoman called Eileen Halpenny. Born in Scotstown, County Monaghan, she was educated at the convent of St Louis. Upon arriving in London for the first time, she initially worked for the Ambassadors' Theatre as a secretary and gradually climbed the ladder. Within three years, she was appointed manager of the theatre – the first woman to occupy such a high position in London's West End – in 1950. When interviewed by a newspaper reporter, she commented that she was 'caught up in the web of the theatre, it was the homeliness and friendship shown to [me] at the Ambassadors' that convinced [me] that theatre was [my] life.'[100]

WHITE-COLLAR WORK

In the 1950s, around 1.5 million women in Britain worked as either secretaries or typists, at a time when just 3 per cent of people in these jobs were men. It was the time that calculating machines and typewriters gradually became a common sight in offices and factories, and this transformed clerical and manual work in a more efficient and accurate way. Working as a typist didn't require a degree but it was considered to be a relatively attractive job. Working in an office was something of a novelty for many women, and London offices eagerly recruited those who could speak English.

In August 1950, three Irish secretaries were rewarded by the British Government for 'all their hard work'. On 4 August 1950, the *Irish Independent* reported that Eileen Brady, who had been secretary to the Lloyd-George family for thirty years, received a silver compact on behalf of the other secretaries of the Houses of Parliament. The newspaper article also noted the great work done by other Irish secretaries. Miss Shea and Miss Blake both worked for the House of Lords, the Dukes of Portland and Devonshire respectively. They had held the same position for more than twenty years.

Irishwomen worked in schools, supermarkets, post offices and banks, amongst other industries, and contributed in all fields and walks of life. They had much better access to white-collar work than their male counterparts in those days.

TRADE UNIONS

A Catholic priest noted in 1836 in the *Catholic Herald* that Irish people were more inclined to take part in trade unions, organisations or secret societies compared to their British counterparts. From its inception, trade unions in Britain had always had regional secretaries and leading activists with an Irish background.

In 1952, there were 9.5 million trade union members in Britain. While it is unknown how many Irish people were included in this number, it is believed that a considerable number of Irish people – both men and women – were involved with all kinds of activities for better conditions and pay.

Jim Duggan from County Waterford came to London in 1954. He was a dedicated trade union activist all through his life and belonged to various groups, such as the Connolly Association.

He was also one of the founder members of the Camden Federation of Residents and Tenants Association. He worked with Irish trade unionists for a couple of decades and observed:

> The Irish are good at organising unions. Ireland was occupied for a long time and we were always fighting against injustice. Because Irish people suffered a lot, we have political understandings and a better understanding on Trade Unions.[101]

Another immigrant also echoed his sentiments:

> … Irish people arrived here well aware that they were the foreigners, the outsiders. They had no illusions about England being the Mother Country. Others came from the Commonwealth, the West Indians feeling that they were owed a living. They'd been told that this was their country, that they were British. The Irish had no such expectations.[102]

Trade unions in Britain have a long history. although the trade union initiative generally became more visible, organised and intense from the late 1960s. Historically and traditionally, the majority of general labouring work in Britain was done by Irish people. These jobs were often dangerous and poorly paid, and the workers lived in appalling conditions. It is no coincidence, therefore, that Irish workers were an integral and valuable part of trade unionism in Britain. A significant post-war development was the increased interest amongst white-collar workers, in both the public and private sectors, in trade unionism.

There were many different trade unions that made a considerable difference to Irish people's lives all through the post-war period.

When it was established in 1922, the Transport and General Workers' Union, or TGWU, was the largest trade union in England. It became known as the Amalgamated Transport and General Workers Union, as it was consolidated with the Docks Group, Waterways Group,

Administrative, Clerical and Supervisory Group, and Passenger Services and Road Transport Group.

Jim Duggan, who worked as an electrical assistant and an electrician, joined the Electrical Trades Union on his arrival in London in 1954. He acknowledged that Irish people who worked for London Transport were all active trade union members: 'The LT, the NHS and many other hospitals in London and across Britain relied heavily on the Irish people's expertise and willingness to work long, unsocial hours in often poorly paid employment.'[103]

The east end of London, where the port of London was located, supported a substantial number of Irish workers and their families for many generations. They were known to be the key workforce in the building of nineteenth-century docklands and some major strikes were organised during this period. Since that time, Irish immigrants had been moving into the area and working as general labourers and dock workers.

Irish dock workers were actively engaged in the Dock, Wharf, Riverside and General Labourers Unions, which was originally established in 1889. It dissolved in 1922 and merged with the TGWU, which emerged in response to the London Dock Strike in 1889. The National Amalgamated Stevedores and Dockers also contained many Irish workers.

Under the wartime scheme, a refusal to work overtime was an offence, but the conflict did give dockers in Britain some form of economic security. The Chief Officer of the Docks Group in London in 1954 was a vigorous Catholic Irish man called Timothy O'Leary, who had a lifetime's experience in the Port of London.

A large-scale dock strike occurred in October 1954 in response to the decision to employ Indian seamen, and nearly 13,000 people joined the movement. Approximately 1,000 of 3,000 ship repair workers were involved with a second strike – this time as a protest against threatened redundancy – which involved a 2-mile march along the Thames, from the East End to a mass meeting at Custom House Fields. These strikers were from shipyards from Tilbury to Teddington.

The National Union of General and Municipal Workers was established in 1924 as a result of a series of mergers. Its members worked in the
gas, electricity and cable-making industries originally, but the union soon
began recruiting from other industries and areas such as iron and steel
building, chemicals and rubber, food and drink, textiles, and shipbuilding.

The National Union of Railwaymen, or NUR, was set up for
railway, guards and platform workers. In 1945, the NUR had more
than 400,000 members, which made it the fifth largest union in
Britain, but its membership fell to around 370,000 in 1956. During
its most active period, it had a publication called the *Railway Review*.

Founded in 1897, The Transport Salaried Staffs' Association,
or TSSA, is for white collar and office workers such as administrative,
managerial, professional and technical workers in the railway, London
Underground, the travel trade, ports and ferries. Its head office is
located near Euston Station. At its peak in the early 1950s, it had more
than 91,500 members.

Although it is not an actual trade union, the Westminster Association
of Catholic Trade Unionists in London was actively catering to the
needs of Catholic trade unionists. Inaugurated by Cardinal Griffin in
November 1946, the main purpose of the association was to assist and
safeguard Catholic trade unionists and spread the charity of Christ
amongst Catholic workers. It also campaigned to end communist
activities. In 1950, its membership increased to 32,000. With its aim
to protect the interests of Irish workers, it opened a liaison office in
Dublin in 1950 so that young Irish workers coming to England could
share some information before crossing the Irish Sea.

THE CONNOLLY ASSOCIATION

The vast majority of Irish Catholics in Britain supported the Labour
Party, as the Irish have traditionally belonged to the working class.
The post-war years saw the rapid growth of various political groups
and politics became higher profile.

It was the height of the Cold War and anti-communism sentiment was running high. People from all walks of life became politically motivated and active in their own beliefs and ideologies.

The Connolly Association, or CA, was founded in London in 1938 to work for the freedom of the Irish people from British rule. Originally called the Connolly Club, which was named after a socialist republican James Connolly and its primary aim was to end partition and work with the British Trade Union and Labour movement for the interests of Irish migrant workers in Britain.

Irish people in London clearly showed a great interest in their activities. For instance, sales of the CA's newspaper, the *Irish Democrat*, dramatically increased during the 1950s. Moreover, all kinds of politically motivated meetings were held in Hyde Park every Sunday afternoon and always attracted a huge crowd, which contained not only Irish people but other immigrants. Around this time, the CA stepped up its trade union involvement and published various pamphlets aimed specifically at trade union members. A report called *Irishmen Make Good Trade Unionists* was a part of the CA's attempts to persuade the trade union movement to tackle issues of concern to the Irish community.

The Catholic Church had historically been hostile to all kinds of movements such as Chartism, the Republican Movement and communism. The Church was adamantly against communism and its attitude was complex, as it had been with other movements. Some people believed that Irish workers were coming under the influence of communists, despite the fact that the English and Irish hierarchies ensured in 1957 that the majority of Irish workers on building sites and road building projects in Britain remained faithful to their Catholic religion. According to various media accounts at that time, the high number of 'very Irish surnames and Christian names of those who were arrested for violence' were as a result of communist-related activities.

The Irish community was split in two. There were some people who went with the flow or turned communists due to peer pressure.

The Anti-Partition League was also against communists and it banned them from membership. According to a statement issued by the Central Executive Council of the Anti-Partition League:

> The annual conference carried by a large majority an executive motion giving power to the Central Executive Council to debar from membership of the League Communists and members of other organisations designated by the Central Executive Council ... The motion aimed immediately at the Connolly Association whose activities were described in the course of the debate as consistently following the Communist Party line.[104]

4

SUPPORT SYSTEMS

*London is the loneliest place I have known: this lone-
liness is the only holy thing in the city.*

Patrick Kavanagh[105]

A network of family and friends is a lifeline in times of crisis, and Irish groups had an abundance of help on which to rely from all across Britain during the post-war years. Scores of organisations were set up in London to meet Irish people's specific needs as the flow of immigrants continued.

Prosperous London during the 1950s had thriving post-war rec-reations for all. Irish pubs, dancehalls and other Irish events played a major role in order to establish a sense of identity and community in a foreign country.

Some of the active and popular groups which functioned as a social lubricant were the Gaelic League, the Gaelic Athletic Association, the Irish Club, the Irish Literary Society, the Anti-Partition League, county associations and various music, dance and parish centre social clubs. They also offered practical and moral support when necessary, and fun and entertainment. It also functioned as a safe haven when being Irish was not easy at times. Nuns and priests were involved with every part of the migrants' settling down process.

A typical Sunday for the majority of Irish people began with attending mass, and then – usually as a large group – they went to the pub or social club and later onto the dancehall.

THE CHURCH

Irish people have had something of a love-hate relationship with church. While many were dedicated and regular Churchgoers, finding the Church both spiritually and socially rewarding, others left Ireland to get away from dominating priests and stifling Catholic dogma for independent careers and life of their own, or perhaps in search of a husband or wife. Despite this, however, many of them didn't completely abandon their religious beliefs, but brought their Catholicism to London with them, and practised in a different context.

Paddy Fahey was one of those people who left Ireland to escape the pressures of religion: 'I was glad to get out of Ireland. The religion drove me out and that was true for a lot of people. They found the religion suffocating.'[106]

Jim Duggan also echoed the sentiments:

I was born into a Catholic family but I rejected the form of Catholicism. I am not religious at all. I don't condemn it. Some people find it necessary but I just don't. I disagree with it basically. After coming here, I didn't join any Irish organisations, or county associations, because they were all taking part in Catholic Church activities.[107]

Taking into account this religious background, it was not unusual that some people carried bitter feelings towards the Church when they left home:

They [bishops] haven't a clue about what it was like having to go, what Irish people had to suffer, jumping on the back of a wagon, driving miles in the open in the depth of winter, going into bad digs.

Young girls, lads were never taught anything, sex or nothing. If you
mentioned sex, it'd be 'get away, don't mention sex, the priest will kill
us all' ... I often wonder, coming from the heart of the heather, how
we survived.[108]

There was a slightly controversial article in the *Catholic Herald*
on 19 November 1954 headlined 'Don't blame clerical interference: Vanishing Irish is only an illusion'. According to the article,
a book called *The Vanishing Irish*, a compilation of essays edited and
written by Fr O'Brien along with other writers, had been published. The book analysed Irish immigrants and pointed out that,
contrary to popular belief, Irish people were not leaving because of
the Catholic Church but due to economic and other social reasons.

The Church's puritanism – along with its constant interference
with dances and other forms of amusement that brought young men
and women together – discouraged marriage. There was no shortage of people who fervently blamed the Church for frowning on
romance. One of them, Sir Shane Leslie, observed other Catholic
countries and noted: 'Sunday in all other Catholic countries is court-
ing time. In Ireland, however, the men and women are kept carefully
on different sides of the church.'

Fr O'Brien also knew that the desire for opportunities to marry
was one of the chief reasons for young people choosing to emigrate,
although he was of the opinion that young Irish women and men
had acquired a 'morbid distaste for marriage'. In any case, it was a hard
time to be a Catholic and Irish at the same time.

Along with the immigrant exodus, there had been some reports
and rumours in Ireland that Irish immigrants lost their religion upon
arriving in agnostic England. Catholic priests' greatest fear was that
their fellow Irish people would become Anglicised and pagan. As a
consequence, the Bishop of Kerry, Dr Moynihan, came to England in
1957 to find out for himself. But he only discovered that 95 per cent
of them were 'doing well' and found that widespread loss of religious
faith was greatly exaggerated.[109]

The Catholic Church had an ulterior motive for its concern for Irish immigrants in England. On top of losing their faith, there was a great concern amongst clergy members that Irish people were at risk of becoming involved with communism and/or the Connolly Association.

Regardless, they often advised Irish Catholics in Britain that they should remain in contact with the Irish clergy and encouraged them to go to their national clubs, by announcing that 'the tendency of some Irish young people to go to English pubs and dancehalls instead of being loyal to the Irish dances, games and functions arranged for them by the parish is a problem'.[110]

Even though many felt uncomfortable with the Church's authority back home, once they had moved to London, it had a whole different meaning and purpose. The Church was described 'like a lamp to moths, the attraction,'[111] and it was not just a place to worship but also an essential place of entertainment as well as being a vital community. Newly arrived Irish immigrants found it uplifting to 'see bright candles, lights, beautiful paintings, colourful stained glasses of a church building, which mitigated the harsh reality in a foreign land.'[112]

Due to the number of Irish people arriving en masse, Irish churches and priests could not accommodate all of the newcomers. They built adjacent social halls and parish centres, which were often used for the congregation, other ceremonies and events. In the name of fundraising, dance and social events were held, often with singers or musicians and the entrance fees were used for fixing or repairing walls or roofs, building a school for children or a house for priests. Those clubs often cleared the debts of many churches and raised necessary funds by selling alcohol; once that debt was paid, however, they suddenly closed the bar.

Regardless, it seems that Irish people needed their church to be the centre of their community:

There are two institutions the Irish can't do without: the pub and
the Church. The area around St. George's in Southwark was a colony.
It was an Irish ghetto, really because it was a Catholic cathedral
though it was bombed out to a shell in 1941. The Irish always settled
around their churches, as the Italians did later on. It was also safety
in numbers when it wasn't safe to be a Catholic ... I remember the
Oblate Fathers that were up in Kilburn; they did tremendous work.
Apart from their spiritual duties, they organised hurling, Gaelic football,
social events and other outings. The Church was the main organiser
of social functions.[113]

Fr Seamus Fullam also appreciated the social role of the Church,
noting: 'After work and at weekends, the men could come and play
cards or darts and socialise with other people. The clubs also kept
them in contact with the Church and their duties.'[114]

As well as being the main organiser of social functions, there were
normally about seven or eight Oblate Fathers in a church and most
of their work was dealing with the affairs of Irish immigrants; they
often organised fun events in an effort to keep the Irish in the Church.
The Commission on Emigration and Other Population Problems
warned that mushrooming Church-run centres, institutions and clubs
in England could become magnets for immigrants as powerful as the
Irish centres in the US in the nineteenth and early twentieth centuries.

With the increasing number of Irish immigrants who swarmed
London churches, the Church desperately tried to acquire more
priests. There was an article headlined 'More Priests Needed for
Southwark' in the *Irish Independent* on 16 April 1951. It claimed that a
conservative estimate put the number of Catholics in the Southwark
Diocese at 230,000; and concluded that at least twenty priests should
be ordained each year.

Archbishop of Westminster Cardinal Griffin, who was of Irish
descent, took a keen interest in the building and rebuilding Catholic
schools during the post-war reconstruction years. He also donated
£1,000 for building the Irish Centre in Camden.

In an attempt to engage with the endless flow of Irish immigrants, Cardinal Griffin visited the Irish Club in Eaton Square in September 1955 and gave a speech:

> Though you have been open for some years, I think it is fitting that this official ceremony should take place in 1955, which I am confident will go down in history as the year in which all the Catholics of this country got together in a supreme effort to help with regard to the problems arising from Irish immigration. This year has seen the opening of several new hostels for immigrants. And it has seen the launches of the great campaign of Irish Missions. I can assure you that I shall spare no effort to see that our Irish brethren are always at home within the Catholic community in this country.[115]

Some of the major Roman Catholic churches in London that were constantly packed with Irish people were: St Augustine's (Hammersmith); The Sacred Heart (Quex Road, Cricklewood); St Thomas' of Canterbury (Fulham); St Bonifaces (Tooting); St Mary Magdalen's (Wandsworth); Notre Dame (Camden Town); and Lady Margaret (Kentish Town); St Patrick's Church (Soho), to name a few.

St Gabriel's in Archway was built by Irish workers under John Murphy. There was a social club a couple of yards away, which was used for weddings, christenings and other social events on Saturday and Sunday.

The Passionist Fathers founded St Joseph's church and retreat on Highgate Hill in 1858 where their congregation increased rapidly with the influx of Irish migrant workers and immigrants into the area. The Catholic community in London was expanding because of the new railways. After the Second World War, an increased Roman Catholic population led to extra masses. The congregation was full of Irish nurses working and living at the nearby Whittington Hospital in the post-war years. During this time, a social club was established, organising Irish dancing in order to keep Irish culture alive and immigrants together.

The Sacred Heart on Quex Road in Cricklewood was always overflowing with newly arrived Irish people in the 1950s, to such an

Quex Road Pioneers outing. The outing was organised by the church of the Sacred Heart in Quex Road, Kilburn. A group of youngsters dance on their return from Clacton-on-Sea.

extent that Mass had to be broadcast over a PA system for those who couldn't get in. Newspaper articles often reported that the church was completely full throughout the whole Sunday.

> From early morning until 1 p.m. there was a Mass every hour. The double closing-services of the women's mission began at 2 p.m. and ended at 5 p.m. Half an hour later, the men's mission began; two services which kept the church packed until 8:30 p.m. The missioners are the Irish Jesuits.[116]

Another nearby church, Our Lady of Hal in Camden Town, was also overflowing with Irish immigrants.

> At night the street outside the church is blocked by the crowds waiting to get in and then again when they crush their way out. This mission

literally stops the traffic. Although the service is held twice nightly, lines of men have to stand all the way down the aisles.[117]

St Agnes in Cricklewood also had a large Irish contingent among its parishioners. The *Irish Independent* reported on 10 April 1950 that all churches in London were overwhelmed with massive crowds, especially at the Holy Week services that had by far surpassed any other year. For instance, Fr James Stevenson noted that almost 1,000 people flocked into the church for the Stations of the Cross on Friday afternoon, when a special Passion sermon was preached by the Revd W. Peers Smith. The church, however, had been built to accommodate just 400.[118]

St Patrick's church in Soho is one of the oldest Roman Catholic churches in Britain. As the first church dedicated to St Patrick in Britain, it was opened in 1792 and ever since its earliest days, the church has been a spiritual centre for the Irish in London. There has always been a heavy concentration of Irish immigrants coming to this church, and this was especially noticeable when times were bad back home. Since the majority of them were destitute, the church – conveniently located in the city centre, within walking distance of one of the most notorious and earliest Irish ghettos – offered them not just spiritual guidance but also hot meals.

The Church of the Most Holy Trinity in Bermondsey has always had a strong Irish tradition. Located amongst the tanneries, wharves and factories of London's Dockhead, the church, along with the presbytery and a Pugin-designed convent, was destroyed in the Blitz and rebuilt in 1959 with seating for approximately 900 people. This is the oldest post-Reformation church in South London and Irish people were always part of it – as the saying goes: 'the pennies of the Irish have been collected'.[119] The church was in one of London's biggest parishes. There were a great many Gaelic speakers in the congregation and the church began the tradition of an annual Gaelic-language service for St Patrick's Day in the early 1900s.

St Mary's church in East Finchley was built as the first post-war Catholic church in the Westminster diocese. Cardinal Griffin laid the foundation stone in 1952. The church was built of brick with a roof of red Italian pantiles and it can accommodate 350 people.

Hammersmith in west London has long been home to a sizeable Irish community. Nazareth House on Hammersmith Road, a care home, employed Irish nurses and these young women – along with many nurses from the hospitals in the area – were a common sight at nearby St Augustine's church and Holy Trinity Brook Green. The latter had a social club, established by a young priest at Holy Trinity, Fr John Crowley, and it was always filled with young Irish people.

An immigrant who worked in Hammersmith remembered:

> There were lots of Irish people but also English people going to Holy Trinity Church as well. But there were a high percentage of Irish people going to their social club. Because the social club was established by the Irish people for the Irish people. There was definitely a need for a place where Irish people could meet, dance and exchange information. Holy Trinity Church was more refined, if you like, and St Augustine was called the Irish Church. Irish social clubs in the 1950s used to be all packed. At the St Augustine parish centre, there were regular bands at weekends.[120]

St Augustine's church was built in 1916. The church and its social club were always overflowing with Irish nurses, who worked nearby. Its weekly individual contribution was 3d in 1952.

Dubliner Fr Roland in Holy Trinity (predecessor to Fr Jim Kylie) set up the Irish Advice Centre at the back of St Augustine, as well as a youth hostel for young Irish men in Hammersmith Grove. Newcomers could stay for up to six weeks in this large hostel and Fr Roland also helped them find a job.

> Getting a room in an Irish house, owned by the Irish, wasn't difficult. It was in fact easy to find a room as well, if you are prepared. But English houses were very difficult with a card on the windows saying, 'No Blacks, No Irish'... Fr. Roland was a chairman of the Irish

Advice Centre. He was a great chap. He helped lots of Irish people.
If somebody dies and he has no money, he always found the money
to bury him.[121]

Frederick Henry Boland, the Irish Ambassador in London between
1950 and 1956, acknowledged that the people who were most
concerned about emigrant welfare were members of the Catholic
clergy – but their concerns were more about spiritual rather than
material welfare; they were especially keen to counteract the influence of the Connolly clubs and the Communist Party.[122]

In 1955, Cardinal Griffin and the Irish hierarchy issued pastoral
letters on emigration in Ireland and urged Irish parents to prepare their
children for emigration. In September 1955, Irish missionary priests
officially began to conduct missions for Irish immigrants in Britain.

The large influx of Irish migrant workers meant there was an urgent
need for their children's schooling. On 2 February 1953, the *Catholic
Herald* reported that the Southwark diocese raised £129,000 within
nine months in order to build sixty schools.

According to his Lenten pastoral letter, Bishop of Southwark, Cyril
Conrad Cowderoy, was concerned that the clergy and laity of the
Southwark diocese were facing enormous school burdens, which
already had 133 aided schools or departments, as well as 150 other
schools of various kinds.

A plethora of religious communities offered sites for schools and
the bishop was planning to build brand new schools as well as
to rebuild existing ones. Various newspaper articles reported that
Our Lady's Convent in Norwood had become an aided secondary school; the Holy Family Convent at Tooting, an independent
grammar school for nearly fifty years, was seeking aided status
as a secondary modern school to help the children of the area;
the Sacred Heart Convent at Honor Oak was to become an aided
primary school; the Sisters of La Sainte Union des Sacres Coeurs
offered to provide a girls' modern school at Bexleyheath; La
Retraite Convent at Clapham Park was providing an aided primary

school; the Religious of St Andrew at Streatham and the Society of the Sacred Heart at Roehampton had given their parish schools to the diocese, to name a few.

Concerned priests in Ireland travelled to London on a regular basis to give services and some advice to Irish workers. For instance, two Jesuits from Dublin were in London for a fortnight in October 1952 to preach at the church of St Aloysius in the Euston/King's Cross area. The first week was a mission for women, who filled all the floor space and galleries every evening. The same service was offered to men on the second week and the church was again packed every evening; it was simply not possible to accommodate all people at once.[123]

In November 1953, the biggest rally ever in Westminster Cathedral was held, with Cardinal Griffin presiding. The Jesuits also visited at St Monica's in Hoxton, St Peter's Woolwich, St Mary of the Angels in Bayswater, St Paul's in Clerkenwell and the area of Camden Town. Fr Patrick Foley noted that the crowds attending the services were getting bigger and bigger each year and that all available seating had been requisitioned from the youth club next door.

In 1955, Catholic organisations opened a couple of hostels for Catholic immigrants in London. Cardinal Griffin was a big supporter of Irish newcomers and also a regular visitor at the Irish Club in Eaton Square. On 30 September 1955, he declared the year 1955 should be remembered because:

> All the Catholics of this country got together in a supreme effort to help with regard to the problems arising from Irish immigration ... I shall spare no effort to see that our Irish brethren are always at home within the Catholic community in this country.[124]

As there was an overwhelming demand for Catholic priests, nuns and social workers to help the Irish community, these groups spent more time outside the Church or the religious institutions. Without the omnipresent support system provided by Catholic priests or lay people, the Irish community would not have survived.

One of the most visible organisations in London in those days was the Legion of Mary. It was founded by Frank Duff in 1921 in Dublin as a lay Catholic organisation whose members give service to the Church on a voluntary basis. They shortly established themselves in London and worked to assist and give guidance for Irish immigrants.

By 1959, between 50 and 80 per cent of people joining the Legion in England and Wales were originally from Ireland. At dawn, Legionaries members waited at main stations such as Euston to meet new arrivals from Ireland. Fr Aedan McGrath said: 'British railway officials are pleased with this work. It is all the more heroic as the trains come so early in the morning.'[125] Fr Eamon Gaynor, who ministered in London to the 250,000 Irish workers in various trades also said: 'There are some undoubtedly who are careless. But there is no group of emigrants anywhere in the world more faithful to the practice of their religion than ours.'[126]

Among the good works performed by Catholic priests and nuns was visiting prisons. Their help and encouragement for prisoners was indispensable. Church people worked hard to keep the fellow country people away from 'the many pagan tendencies in Britain and of the moral outlook totally different in many ways from that of their own land'.[127] The great majority of the people ended up in prison due to excessive drinking and the consequences of it, such as fighting and petty crimes. Irish people who got involved with organised crime were actually rare. 'These people do not lose their faith and it is generally not difficult to get them to the sacrament,' said a prison chaplain.[128]

In the same manner, Irish nurses faithfully practised their religion at their work. However, Provost William O'Grady, parish priest of Our Lady and St George in Walthamstow, and chaplain to Whipps Cross Hospital in Leytonstone, complained that general hospital facilities for Mass were inadequate, referencing an incident in which the hospital management committee refused to give Catholic nurses permission to attend a special early Mass on Sundays at Walthamstow.

In response, he stopped leading Mass at the hospital on 17 May 1953 and demanded that the hospital management committee provide a private room big enough to hold the services. There were approximately 300 nurses who wished to attend services in the small Protestant chapel, but many of them couldn't get in and had to kneel outside in the cold. O'Grady, in a rather threatening manner, urged:

> I have tried hard to meet the hospital management committee by asking if the staff can have extra time off to attend services at my church, and have offered to say a special Mass at 6 a.m. All we ask is freedom to carry on our religion without interference … I have warned the authorities that I am in a position to block the flow of nurses from Ireland, and if they persist in their interference with religious liberty all recruitment of Irish Catholic girls will stop.[129]

Although it is unclear whether he resumed saying Mass again or not, as the letter above suggests, Catholic priests were generally in authoritative positions within British hospitals.

CATHOLIC INSTITUTIONS

Irish nuns and sisters were involved with all aspects of life such as teaching, helping with employment services, looking after the 'unfortunate' (pregnant women, babies and unmarried mothers, to name just a few groups), providing houses, shelters, medical facilities and nurseries, all the while dedicating themselves to religious life.

ST BRIGID'S, HAMMERSMITH

St Brigid's convent in Hammersmith was the focal point of the London mission of the Irish Sisters of Charity, or the Religious Sisters of Charity, between 1920 and 1998. The Sisters not only looked after the sick and the unfortunate in six immediate parishes; they also ran guilds and sodalities and instructed converts. Their institution eventually moved to Mater Dei in Hammersmith Grove, from where the sisters ran an Irish Welfare Centre and helped find accommodation for Irish immigrants.

The sisters also worked for various other local charities, such as the Westminster Crusade of Rescue, an English Catholic charity that provided assistance to pregnant Irishwomen. Hundreds of thousands of Irish women travelled to Britain to give birth and between 1950 and 1953, nearly 2,000 Irish women applied for support. Cardinal Griffin also acknowledged that Irish girls who became pregnant had 'too great a fear' of the Irish clergy and that 'too narrow a view' was taken of the offence in Ireland.[130] A report presented to a meeting of British charities found that 'a girl has little chance of going free under almost two years' from Irish Mother and Baby homes.

ST JOSEPH'S HOSPICE

Located on Mare Street in Hackney, north-east London, St Joseph's Hospice was founded in 1905 by Fr Peter Gallwey, who became Provincial of the English Province of the Society of Jesus. Fr Gallwey, from County Kerry, was the rector of Street Jesuit Mission. With the help of Sisters of Charity from Ireland, the staff initially worked by visiting the sick and the unfortunate in their own homes, but they quickly realised that there were more that needed to be done in the gas-lit squalor. He therefore built the hospice so that the poor who suffered and died in the disease-ridden East End of London could have a 'place to die in peace'.

In 1922, three new wards and a new laundry were added. Facing unceasing demand for healthcare services in the area, the building was extended to provide space for seventy-five extra patients, and in addition, a chapel was constructed. During the Second World War, the hospice served as a parish church after the neighbouring church, St John the Baptist's, was bombed. The hospice's in-patient beds were able to accommodate up to 500 people by 1957. The brand new wards were purposely built for terminally ill patients, with a view of the outside world.

In October 1957, the Archbishop of Westminster opened a new wing and praised the huge amount of work the Irish Sisters of Charity put into the hospice: 'despite the welfare state, Catholic work of love for the dying was never so necessary as today'.

Over the decades, uninterrupted demand for beds resulted in constant extensions, and nuns from Ireland arrived in droves to work as nurses. Apart from teaching in local schools and caring for the terminally ill, the hospice also provided care for older people in St Patrick's wing, and food and clothes for poor people who continuously visited the hospice on a daily basis.

ST MARY'S CONVENT, WALTHAMSTOW

St Mary's Convent was founded in Walthamstow as a missionary centre in 1921. The sisters visited and looked after the sick, organised guilds and sodalities for girls and boys. In 1931, St Mary's became the primary school for the residential children and children of the parish. The institution gradually expanded each year and in 1950, a new school was opened.

THE RELIGIOUS SISTERS OF MERCY

The Religious Sisters of Mercy was founded in 1831 by Catherine McAuley, who used an inherited fortune to build a House of Mercy in Dublin. The institution provided religious, educational and social services for poor and unfortunate women and children. Other institutions soon mushroomed in Britain; other Sisters of Mercy schools in London included St Edward's, Lisson Grove, Marylebone; St Catherine's School, Twickenham; and St Joseph's Convent School, Wanstead, East London.

CATHOLIC CLUBS

Founded in 1906 by Margaret Fletcher, the Catholic Women's League consisted of predominantly Irish members. Regular events were held throughout the 1950s at the Royal Albert Hall, with the support and help of Cardinal Griffin.

Elizabeth Fitzgerald compiled a report to explain the dire state of Irish girls and women's welfare in Britain. Fitzgerald was president of the archdiocese of Westminster branch of the Catholic Women's League and she was concerned 'at the numbers of young, ignorant and untrained girls arriving from Ireland to swell the ranks of unmarried mothers'.[131] As the English and Irish Catholic charities were overwhelmed and couldn't cope with all of them, Irish girls were often cared for by non-Catholic organisations and their babies were adopted by non-Catholic families. Although her report was quite influential, the organisation did not have specific programmes to support Irish immigrants.

To cater for Catholic men, Cardinal Griffin opened the Challoner Club in September 1949. The club was considered as the one and only national social centre for Catholics at that time. In mid-1950, when a spectacular opening party was organised, it attracted 4,000 paid members and this number continued to swell. By January 1952, the *Catholic Herald* reported that the club's amenities were also keeping up along with the expanding members.

The premises were located at 59-61 Pont Street in Chelsea and cost approximately £6,000. The address had previously been the home of the Faun Club and the Pont Street Bridge Club.

The Challoner Club Committee shortly acquired the adjoining property, the wartime home of the Danish legation. After many alterations and much redecoration, the building was joined to the original establishment. The religious institution included residential accommodation for fifteen visitors with single and double beds; a large banqueting hall which could be used for private parties such as dinners of former pupils of Catholic colleges; a buttery; a dining room in the basement where members could enjoy light refreshment; a library and a music room, where committee members arranged frequent concerts and lectures. The club had its own Challoner orchestra, which consisted of twenty musicians. It also organised regular dances, music, dramatic and sporting events and pilgrimages. In September 1950, around 350 people went to Rome on the club's holy year pilgrimage. The club also conducted regular Barcelona pilgrimage trips.

In the midst of the most rapid expansion of the Irish immigrant population, a serious mission to help the vulnerable newcomers had started. In order to protect them from 'pagan England', a committee was formed to address the specific problems faced by Irish people.

The London Irish Centre – the vision of Fr Tom McNamara from County Cork – was officially opened on 27 September 1955. Its purpose was to promote the social, recreational and spiritual welfare of Irish people in London. The centre provided temporary but decent lodgings for men and women and a hall for social functions, until they were able to find their own arrangements.

Within walking distance of Euston station, allegedly 'the farthest an Irishman can walk with two full suitcases', the Irish Centre soon became a lifeline for Irish immigrants or the last resort to some. The people who did not know where to go or what to do upon getting off the train often came to the centre directly, as they were typically given the address of the centre by the Legion of Mary at the docks before taking a boat.

The centre spent £15,000 on a chapel and £10,000 on a hall for social and cultural activities. Various people and organisations, including Cardinal Griffin and Arthur Guinness and Son Ltd, donated a substantial amount of money to the centre.

A newspaper reporter interviewed some of its very first residents:

Kevin, aged 24, a lathe operator, told me how he came to be the first of five residents already in the house. On reaching London he found the lodgings recommended to him quite hopeless. Advice from a parish priest led him to Father McNamara who was only just on the point of moving into the new Centre himself. Kevin went with him. Robert, a carpenter and Pat, a draughtsman told me that the Centre gave them their first comfortable night in London. 'All right now.' When I asked them how they felt about the future and if they were happy, Robert said: 'The happiness I have found so far is thanks to this place.' And Pat said: 'I've got a job now and I'm looking round for my own place to live, of course. I think I'm going to be all right in England now.'[132]

Another organisation with very similar aims, the Irish Chaplaincy in Britain, was established in 1957 in order to cater to the needs of Irish people in a multicultural urban environment. It co-operated with other churches and welfare agencies. Fr Bobby Gilmore, who served as a chaplain, summarised: 'the psychological journey of migration takes far longer than the geographical one.'

PUBS AND CLUBS

The pub has long been considered the ultimate Irish institution. Typical male migrant workers spent far more time in the pub than their often-dreary accommodation. Because it was the hub of community life, people went along not just for drinks and craic, but with the purpose of obtaining information about jobs and accommodation, doing business and getting paid. An Irish navvy in London, for example, had to make a regular appearance to find about the job situation: 'I hung around until the pubs opened. It is not for the sake of the drink I went in but in the hope of hearing about some job that might be going.'[133]

Some people visited the pub with a purpose, while other men seemed to be there perpetually, except for when they were either working or sleeping. In fact, that was the only world they knew – especially the rural, young men without formal education. The essence of the life of a typical navvy in London was captured:

> Nothing affects me so much, I think, as seeing the little groups of Irish
> walking aimlessly around town every Sunday evening with no interest
> in anything at all, the creatures – only waiting for the pubs to open
> … It's hard enough on young Irishmen who were reared out in the
> country to have nowhere to go on their day off except the pubs. It's
> small wonder that we are getting a bad reputation over here.[134]

For those who were habitually hanging out at the pub, publicans somehow acted as authority figures: 'on a par with the priest, the publican is the most influential figure, and the repository of as many secrets.'[135]

The pub also functioned as a 'permanent address'. For example, some people who never stayed in one place as they moved around with work or housing problems often received their letters from home addressed to 'The Crown', the best-known Irish pub in Cricklewood.

Irish navvies' living arrangements were notoriously brutal. It was not uncommon to find ten men sleeping on the floor in a cramped and unhygienic room. Accommodation meant a place to get some sleep, not to stay. Although Paddy Fahey, a professional photographer, was much better off and lucky to have his own room, he described his and many others' routine at that time:

> I had a tiny room with a bed and table and chair, £3 a week. When I finished work at night I had only four bare walls to look at. All the knowledge I ever got was out at the pubs … the form was to drink in the Clarence on Northend Road until 11pm then off to the Hibernian in Fulham as the bands came on late and there was an extension to the bar.[136]

The pubs in Britain functioned differently from those in Ireland and America. Traditional Irish music sessions, which soon became commonplace in many London pubs, originated from patrons meeting and sharing music amongst themselves. Unlike places in American cities where Irish musicians were hired to perform on stage, London sessions were intended to be enjoyed by all people, who were invited to join in – to play or sing spontaneously, and purely for their own edification.

One of the major differences between the Irish and London pubs back in the early 1900s was in the ownership:

> All the London pubs were owned by the breweries, with the Governor's living quarters over the bar. Each pub carried only the beer of the brewery that owned it, thus you had 'A Whitbread House' or A 'Watney House' and so on. In Ireland they were individually owned, by what was commonly called 'The Publican' and the pub's carried different brands of beer or Porter, such as 'Beamish and Crawford' and 'Murphys' of Cork, or 'Guinness' of Dublin.
>
> As I recall, the major physical difference between pubs in London and Dublin or any Irish Town was, the London Pubs were almost all

corner houses, built specially by the Breweries as pubs, with living quarters upstairs. In the Irish case they were generally the ground-floor space in some building in the block. In the London case they were generally more finely finished, with a public bar and a private bar and so forth. Of course some of the Irish ones had their public and private and of course the 'snug' where you went if you didn't want to be seen, particularly the ladies.

The greatest difference would be between the Irish country pubs and the city pubs, the country places were smaller, old, low ceiling places, more informal, with a little short counter for serving. Generally they had a fireplace to provide some heat in the Winter, and sometimes in the Summer. They were generally in the same family for generations, and were the social centres of the community.[137]

Irish pubs were also called spirit groceries as Irish publicans sold groceries and played multi-functional roles all under one roof. In London, on the other hand, there was the enticing music scene.

> We had great music at the Bedford – fiddles, concertinas and tin whistles – and there was hardly a jig or a reel that they didn't play ... This town is, in many ways, more Irish than a lot of the towns at home. More Irish is spoken here and much more Irish music is played here.[138]

The Laurel Tree, Camden, had regular music sessions also and the pub was always packed; it was especially popular at weekends with Gaelic speakers from Connemara. A fiddle player, Bobby Casey from County Clare, regularly played at the Laurel Tree, accompanied by Willie Clancy (also from Clare) on the pipes and a fiddle player, Galway man Martin Byrnes.

Overall, the pubs in London looked better than those back home. Another unmistakable aspect of the London pub was observed by many Irish men: 'The women are as plentiful in the pubs here as there are fleas on a goat and no man can be at ease wherever they are.'[139]

Some Irish people became closely associated with the licensed trade, becoming tenants and managers of many famous London pubs, dancehalls and restaurants. There were many Irish pubs or the pubs that Irish people often frequented. It is impossible to mention all but here is a list of some popular pubs in London at that time.

Brady's pub (Hackney)

Nag's Head (on Holloway Road)

The Crown (Cricklewood)

McGovern's (on Kilburn High Road in Kilburn)

Biddy Mulligan's (Hammersmith)

The Hop Poles (on King Street in Hammersmith; frequented by IRA members)

The Richmond (next to the flat where Michael Collins used to live, on Shepherd's Bush Road in Shepherd's Bush)

The Harp (Fulham)

St Jude's (Islington)

St George's (Elephant and Castle)

The Mother Red Cap (on Holloway Road)

The White Swan (on Wapping High Street)

The Black Cap (Camden)

The Half Moon pub (on Holloway Road in Islington)

Ward's (Piccadilly Circus)

DANCEHALLS

Unlike pubs, which attracted a predominantly male crowd, dance-halls offered a neutral venue for both men and women. Dancehalls were not only the place to dance and have fun without spending a lot of money for young immigrant workers; they also offered the opportunity to meet old and new friends, find jobs and accommodation, and exchange news from home. Dancehalls played a crucial role for immigrants in the process of settling in, which made it easier to face their harsh new reality. It was also the place where

life-changing events took place, as scores of people found their
future spouses there.

Just like pubs, dancehalls were also used as a place to network.
'Quite a bit of business was transacted there, too. In the early days,
if we needed a plumber or an electrician we'd always find one at the
Galty [Galtymore]. It was great big network.'[140]

As soon as Tony arrived in London, he went to a dancehall:

> I went to the dancehall immediately. We were going out dancing and
> meeting lots of people so you can get information. It was very easy
> to find information there. The Banba was my first dancehall I went
> to. I met a girl from Innis there. Her name was Kitty. I used to work
> at the Emerald as a doorman. I was there for eighteen months. It was
> open every night. Those places were always packed with young Irish
> women and men. The owner of the new Emerald made a lot of money,
> then closed down the hall and came back to Ireland. The Garryowen
> made a lot of money as well and the owner bought lots of properties
> in Ireland. The Banba in Kilburn was open seven nights a week as well.
> The ground floor of the Galty was for the traditional Irish dancing,
> ceilidh, and it was open at weekends' night only.[141]

Many people divided their salaries into three categories – rent money,
food money and dance money. For most Irish people, going to a
dancehall was an exciting, if nerve-wracking, ordeal. There was a
strict dress code: men were required to wear a suit with a white shirt
and a tie. There were bouncers at the door at the Gresham who could
offer a tie for a shilling. Women also dressed up for the occasion; for
instance, they wore three-tier stiffened petticoats underneath with
black stockings and beta shoes (flat) or Curtis shoes (high heeled),
or whatever fashion dictated at the time. Nearly every dancehall had
a resident show band often from Ireland and they would play country
and western music.

To many women, it was the highlight of the week; they really
looked forward to dressing up and going to the dancehall. 'The rent

wasn't a lot, but we never ate much. We kept our money for buying dresses and going dancing.'[142]

Eager learners took up the offer of jive and ballroom dancing lessons. Social life revolved around dancing and many people developed a passion for it:

> I remember dressing up for those nights out. Taffeta was in then – red and black taffeta skirts with gold at the bottom. I'd wear a nice top – maybe white, but something nice, something dressy. We used to do a lot of jiving, so we'd wear flat sandals – the ones with the straps up your legs. We'd get very excited dressing up, and of course, we'd walk everywhere. We were saving our money, so we couldn't afford to go by bus.[143]

A group of young boys dance at a Brent Irish Society social event.

Men generally went to the pub to have a couple of pints for some Dutch courage before going to the dancehall, in the hope of talking to girls and dancing with them. A male immigrant recalled:

> You went to the dancehalls to meet people, to talk to girls, and you didn't
> have a hope in hell if you couldn't dance. You were the wall-flower – you
> could sit there all night like Greta Garbo. Fred Astaire and Ginger Rogers,
> who we followed at that time [*sic*]. The dancing in those days was dif-
> ferent. It was romantic, first and foremost. You were in an embrace, you
> were dancing, but there was nothing immoral about it. You might take her
> home – if she liked you and you liked her – and a date was made to go to
> the cinema on Monday night. You might have a kiss and a squeeze, and the
> romance might continue from there. You were terrified of your life of
> having sex! Because if you did, you'd have to get married, and none of the
> fellas could afford to get married no more than I could.[144]

There was no shortage of places where boys meet girls. Added to which, the easy availability of public transport in London gave people, and women in particular, the freedom to move independently when-ever and wherever they wanted. Hence, they were able to attend all kinds of outings and gathering fairly easily.

Here are some of the most popular Irish dancehalls.

THE BLARNEY

Irish dancehalls and ballrooms were often owned by entrepreneurs. Mick Gannon, one of the most high-profile entrepreneurs in 1950s' London, owned the Blarney, which could be found at No.31 Tottenham Court Road. The dancehall was in the basement and upstairs was the Gala Berkeley Cinema, a neat arrangement as people who finished watching a film used to go downstairs to dance. Belinda, who met her husband at the Blarney, remembered: 'There was only one exit downstairs and it was really a scary place.'[145]

Compared to other popular dancehalls, the Blarney was rather orthodox in its business approach. For a start, it did not serve alcohol:

A crowd of eager fans watch a performance by Joe Lynch, a popular Radio Éireann figure, at the Banba Club in 1955.

A popular touring Irish band, the Big Town Showband, at the backstage of the Galtymore or the Banba.

Some halls were very conservative in their outlook and only soft drinks and tea were available on the premises. Even upmarket halls such as the Blarney Club in London's West End, had notices on the wall saying 'No Jiving'. The floor manager at the Blarney Club actually spent most of his time watching for and trying to stop couples jiving. Sometimes a couple would sneak into a darkened corner for a bit of a jive, but old eagle eyes would soon spot them.[146]

THE BANBA

Along with the Galtymore, this was another popular dancehall in Kilburn. Joe Lynch from Radio Éireann, who was extremely popular in those days, often performed here. There was also tea dancing on Sunday afternoons:

> I remember the tea-dances at the Banba Club in Kilburn – a half crown to get in and you'd get a spam sandwich and a cup of tea. On Sundays, that was 3 pm to 6:30 pm, and some of them used to wait and hang on for the evening session from 8 o'clock till 11. They used to do fox-trots, slow waltzes, and that; there was also Irish dancing; the Siege of Ennis and the Walls of Limerick ... Then it was natural to get up and dance, the only social life we ever had was dancing.[147]

THE BOW PALAIS/THE EMERALD BALLROOM

The Embassy Billiard Hall in Bow, east London, was renamed the Bow Palais after the Second World War. It again changed its name to the Emerald Ballroom in 1950 because it hosted frequent events by Irish show bands and Irish dance events, becoming more like an Irish dancehall. The venue was always full, especially with Irish nurses from nearby St Andrew's Hospital. Unfortunately it was severely damaged by fire in 1956 and was forced to close.

THE BUFFALO

The Buffalo was a high-profile dancehall in Camden. Irish people from all over London and towns as far afield as Peterborough habitually came to Camden Town at the weekend. In its early days, the Buffalo didn't have a licensed bar, so everyone would drink in pubs until closing time and then move on to the dancehall. John Fitzgerald, who took over the Brighton pub on Camden High Street in 1957, recalled.

> Irish fellas would come from all over for a night out in Camden Town. They'd come here in holiday time and they'd get off at the station on a Thursday night and they probably wouldn't go back for a week and, when holiday time came again, they'd be in droves in Camden Town. They'd enjoy themselves for a week and they'd dance in the Buffalo and probably fall in love.[148]

It was established by William Joseph Fuller, who came to London as a teenager to work on building sites. He was born in Finogue, approximately 5 miles from Tralee, County Kerry, in 1917. Fuller eventually started his own construction business and with the money he made, bought a rundown Irish club when he was only 20 and transformed it into one of the most successful Irish dancehalls. He once said: 'I love to take risks … Life is a risk.'[149]

During its early days, it was an infamously rough venue with regular fights and all kinds of trouble. Local authorities once closed it down, but tenacious Fuller quickly persuaded the local police chief to reopen it, pledging that he would never need the police again in his club. Also an amateur boxer and wrestler, Fuller kept his word by manning the door himself and transformed the dancehall into a safe, popular venue. This progressive and versatile businessman is considered to be one of the first people to bring rock music from America to Camden Town.

An immigrant himself, Fuller recognised that it was essential to have a place for Irish immigrants where they could meet and socialise. As his business was going well, he subsequently purchased several rundown properties in the 1950s and built a chain of dancehalls in England, eventually expanding his empire into Ireland. He then later developed several Irish dancehalls in American cities, such as

New York, Boston, Chicago, San Francisco and Las Vegas. There was
a saying about this Kerryman at that time: 'What Hitler didn't knock
down, Bill Fuller did.'[150]

As one of the most remarkable Irish entrepreneurs of the century,
Fuller died at the age of 91 in 2008. An obituary paid tribute to him:

> Fuller lived an extraordinary life and will be remembered as an Irish
> gentleman. He always had time for his own people and never lost
> touch with his humble business beginnings. 'I'll keep Camden until
> I move out of this world … It was the first place of my own that I had,
> so I wouldn't dream of parting with it. Camden will never be sold.'[151]

THE EMERALD
Situated close to Hammersmith Hospital, hordes of Irish nurses who
worked in the area were attracted to this dancehall. It was open every
night, with consistently large crowds. Musician Paddy Malynn regularly
played the accordion on Saturday nights. James Conway, a builder, was
the owner of this dancehall. and Tom O'Brian worked as the manager.

THE FORUM
Originally built as an art deco cinema in 1934, this place in Kentish
Town was transformed to an Irish dancehall in the 1950s.

THE FOUR PROVINCES
Previously called the Highbury Palais dancehall, it was on Compton
Avenue in north London. It became the Four Provinces Irish Dancehall
in the 1950s.

THE GALTYMORE
Affectionately called 'the Galty', Irish immigrants considered this place
as the 'sanctuary'. It was one of the most popular and longstanding Irish
dancehalls in Britain. It was located in Kilburn, or County Kilburn as it was
called, because the area had the highest Irish population within London.
To many people, the dancehalls played an essential role in their lives.

Irish wrestlers at the Galtymore in Cricklewood.

A crowd of people enjoy a performance at either the Banba in Kilburn
or the Galtymore Club in Cricklewood.

The Galtymore was an Irish institution. It was ironically probably the only place in Ireland that did not recognise borders or religious differences, even though it was located in Cricklewood. If you were Irish you were Irish and that was it; that was the only criteria needed.[152]

Donegal singing star Margo remembered the Galty:

It really saved lives – people from remote areas of Donegal, Mayo, Galway and Kerry lived for the weekend at the Galtymore. Without that all important Friday and Saturday night, many would have felt totally alone and many would fallen into depression. It was their home from home and kept the spirits high in difficult times.[153]

Scores of show bands travelled from Ireland and played at the Galtymore, even during Lent, while it was prohibited in Ireland. Big

The Royal Showband on stage at the Galtymore where live Irish music and the visiting bands used to attract large audiences.

Tom, Dana, Margo, Brendan Bowyer, Larry Cunningham and Jack Ruane were among the regular show bands. Delia Murphy, Margaret Barry and Bridie Gallagher from County Donegal also sang here often. It was open from 9 p.m. to 2 a.m., weekends only and the ground floor was for traditional Irish dances such as the ceilidh. Some people were lucky enough to find their sweetheart at the Galtymore. Consequently, this was a popular venue for wedding parties.

It was John Byrne from Kilflynn, County Kerry, who opened the dancehall in 1951. The eldest of a family of twelve, who came to London in 1941, this Kerryman with sharp business acumen tried all kinds of events at the dancehall during the height of his career in order to maximise profits by not just inviting all kinds of musicians and organising bingo nights, but also hosting boxing and wrestling matches. His brother, Paddy, was also in the business. In the 1960s, Byrne was invited back to Ireland by former Taoiseach Seán Lemass. With the ample money he made at the Galtymore, Byrne was able to finance building projects, such as the development of Parnell House, a mock-Georgian office block in Dublin. He also set up his own company called Princes Investments, which owned the Brandon Hotel in Tralee.

THE GARRYOWEN
Established by Johnny Muldoon, the Garryowen could be found at Brook Green, on Shepard's Bush Road in Hammersmith. It was 2s to get in and the dancehall was open on Sunday afternoons and evenings. Ruby Molorney was a regular Garryowen's singer.

THE GLOCAMORA
Paddy Casey began the Glocamora in Bayswater with fellow Kerryman Bill Fuller, but Casey later bought him out to become the sole owner.

THE GRESHAM
Located on Holloway Road near Archway in north London and opposite St Gabriel's Catholic church, the building was previously a cinema and became an Irish ballroom in 1959. Close to the Whittington and

Royal Northern hospitals, where countless Irish nurses worked, the place was always crowded. Irish show bands played on a regular basis here.

THE HAMMERSMITH PALAIS
Some people claim that this place is not strictly an Irish dancehall, but the venue was always crowded with Irish people, particularly nurses, who worked at nearby hospitals in Hammersmith.

THE HIBERNIAN
Just like the Galtymore, this was a relatively large-scale Irish dancehall, located in Fulham Broadway. Uilleann piper James Quinn from County Galway, Malachy Sweeney's Ceili Band, fiddle player Sean Maguire and many other musicians played all sorts of music. Margo Barry also played at the inaugural session of Comhaltas Ceoltóirí Éireann (Society of the Musicians of Ireland).

THE INNISFREE
Located in Ealing, west London, this is one of the Irish dancehalls that were established by Paddy Casey from Kerry. He also opened a dancehall called Casey's in Queensway.

THE NATIONAL
Along with the Galtymore and the Banba, another popular venue in the vicinity was the National on Kilburn High Road, which was operated by Kevin Flynn from Sligo.

THE PRIDE OF ERIN
Located on Tottenham Court Road, the fiddler Julia Clifford often played here. During the post-war years, this dance hall was a popular venue for youngsters to enjoy set dancing.

THE ROUND TOWER
It was also located on Holloway Road in Kentish Town. As it was close to the Nag's Head pub, many men used to go there for a couple of pints before going dancing here.

THE SHAMROCK CLUB
Paddy Casey, from Sneem, County Kerry, established this dancehall in Elephant and Castle. One of the most popular and regular show bands at this venue was Doctor Bill Loughnane, with the Tulla Céilí Band.

THE 32 CLUB
This building opposite the Royal Oak pub in Harlesden, north London, was originally the cinema. After the Picardy Theatre closed in 1957, it became an Irish dancehall.

High-profile clubs and groups were purposely established by and for middle-class and professional people to cater to their specific needs and social backgrounds. Here are some of the most active clubs after the war.

THE ERIN MOR SOCIAL CLUB
Erin Mor was established in February 1951 as a club that offered social entertainment, mutual help, mental and moral improvement and rational recreation. A subscription of a few shillings annually was compulsory to join the club.

THE IRISH CLUB
The Irish Club in London's Eaton Square opened in 1947, when several existing Irish clubs came together, such as the Emerald Club – a wartime club for Irish members of the armed forces – and the Four Provinces, both of which had premises in Bloomsbury. Like this brand-new Irish Club, those clubs were non-sectarian and non-political.

With the aid of a donation from the Guinness family, the club was created especially for the movers and shakers of Ireland who were visiting the country, as well as the Irish in Britain. Professionals regularly attended the club along with politicians, journalists, lawyers, artists and aristocrats, but the club also welcomed ordinary people in separate functions or occasions. The club had nearly 2,000 members at one point and its premises consisted of twenty-one guest rooms, a bar, television room, dining room and library.

A group of people at the Forester's dance in Battersea.

Lord Longford, father of renowned historian Thomas Pakenham, or the 8th Earl, was president of the club until his death in 2001. Amongst other high-profile people, Garrett Fitzgerald and Conor Cruise O'Brien frequented the bar. George Bernard Shaw also received an invitation to join to the club but he refused by famously saying: 'I can imagine nothing less desirable than an Irish Club. Irish people in England should join English clubs and avoid each other like the plague. If they flock together like geese they might as well never have left Ireland. They don't admire, nor even like each other.'[154]

A London correspondent for the *Irish Independent* remarked in February 1951 that the opportunities open to Irish people in London for social enjoyment had widened extensively compared with a few years before. All kinds of Irish entertainments were provided every day, with not one vacant date, even during the weeks of Lent. For instance, the Irish Club issued its programme packed with daily events such as debates, gramophone recitals, bridge parties, Gaelic choir singing, concerts and readings.

One of the regular events the club organised was the GAA pre-match function. Occasional elaborate functions included a reception, dinner and concert on Sunday night. Well-known musicians or artists were often invited for the occasion.

In June 1951, residential and catering facilities became a reality at its house at Eaton Square after the Irish Club received a gift of £1,000 by an anonymous benefactor, who visited the club for the first time and expressed great admiration for the arrangements and activities of the club. The Eaton Square premises were closed in 2003.

THE NATIONAL UNIVERSITY OF IRELAND CLUB LONDON

The National University of Ireland (NUI) Club London was founded on 14 February 1929 by Dr T.J. Kiernan while he was Secretary to the Irish High Commissioner in the Irish Embassy in London. His wife, Delia Murphy, a NUI Galway graduate, was co-founder. The NUI London was essentially an exclusive graduate club at which graduates newly arrived in London could meet with fellow graduates from NUI franchises as well as other Irish universities, colleges and institutes of technology. Membership was free and open to all graduates from the NUI, Trinity College, Dublin and Queen's College, Belfast, all of whom were based in London.

The club hosted dinners and social activities throughout the year, including Sunday evening gatherings by inviting musicians or artists. On 20 May 1951, Charles Kennedy from Dublin was invited to perform at a Celtic concert for the members, which attracted a huge crowd. Many NUI members also belonged to the Irish Club, which had the same purpose.

INDEPENDENT CHARITIES AND GROUPS

Charitable organisations and independent groups played a crucial role in supporting Irish people in London.

COMHALTAS CEOLTÓIRÍ ÉIREANN

Comhaltas Ceoltóirí Éireann, or the Society of the Musicians of Ireland, was established in Mullingar, County Westmeath in 1951 in order to promote the traditional music, language and dance of Ireland such as ceilidh and set dancing. It organises an annual Fleadh

Cheoil (Festival of Music) in Ireland as well as in Britain, a Fleadh na Breataine (All-Britain Fleadh Cheoil) and regional Fleadhanna. It promotes music classes such as the accordion, concertina, tin whistle, fiddle, guitar, uilleann pipes, banjo and bodhrán.

Comhaltas Ceoltóirí Éireann London branch started at the Hibernian Club in Fulham where traditional Irish music was often played. The organisation was based at St Augustine's Social Club on Fulham Palace Road. Limerick flute player Paddy Taylor was a member of the founding committee of the west London Comhaltas branch. Other people on the original committee included the piper Michael Daly, John and Joan Burke, Paddy Malynn and Liam Farrell. Paddy Taylor also was one of the founding members of the Irish Traditional Music Association in London.

The first Irish Dance Academy in London was founded by Charles Smyth who came to London from Kilkenny in 1949. Through his dance academy, he helped producing countless leading champion dancers, teachers and adjudicators in England. Smyth and Eileen Ryan were the first people to be registered as a TCRG, or the Irish Dancing Teachers Examination, administered by the governing body of Irish

Young Irish dancers at St Joseph's pose for a photograph with their teacher.

Percival school of Dancing. A group of young girls from the Percival School of Dancing. On the floor in front of them is a trophy and a shield.

dancing, An Coimisiún Le Rincí Gaelacha, in 1949. Dance classes were hugely popular and readily available all across London in the 1950s.

Charlie Smyth taught dances at different venues such as the Killarney Club in Paddington and the Marylebone Evening Institute, and his student dancers were constantly busy performing at the South Bank Exhibition, the prestigious Porchester Hall in Queensway, and various events all over London. When there were music events, the money was always collected for fundraising. For instance, during a dance event at the Porchester Hall in 1951, money was raised to send child competitors to Brum Feis and to make purchases for the camogie team.

Thomas MacMahon from Ballybunion, County Kerry, started a music club called The Killarney Club in 1950. Its members reached almost 500 by 1951. It grew to become one of the most prolific and sought-after groups in the 1950s in London. The club mainly catered for Irish boys and girls in the Paddington District which was affiliated to the London Evening Recreational Institute. Members met in Amberley Road Schools every night except Sundays. The Club had its own pipe band. A.F. Phair, a pipe major of the Irish Guards, was a tutor.

All through the post-war years, there was no shortage of Irish
music and dance events. They were held almost on a daily basis at
numerous venues from small marquees to the Royal Albert Hall.
The Lyric Theatre in Hammersmith was one of the most popular
venues. Originally built as an opera house, called the Lyric Opera
House, in 1895, this crowd-pleasing theatre in west London showed
Irish-themed plays and the plays written by Irish writers during the
1950s. One of the most beloved shows played here was the *Shadow of
a Gunman* by Sean O'Casey.

In the early 1950s, the St Patrick's Day annual Gaelic service was
held at various churches in London and approximately 10,000 Irish
people formed the processions for the event. In 1953, along the route
to the ruins of St George's Cathedral in Southwark where a war-
blitzed statue of St Patrick had been enshrined, hundreds of thousands
of people waited for the procession to come from Whitehall and
across Westminster Bridge. The procession was led by the borough's
Pipe Band, followed by contingents from schools of Irish dancing
in traditional costume and members of the Westminster Youth Club
who wore green sashes. After the crowd went into the cathedral,
the processionists said the Rosary in Irish and heard a sermon in
both Irish and English, followed by Benediction.

IRISH EMBASSY

In July 1950, the Irish government made arrangements to purchase
a mansion at No.17 Grosvenor Place, which would shortly house
the future Irish Embassy. This five-storey mansion of grey stone is
located only a five-minute walk from Hyde Park Corner, one of the
most expensive residential areas of central London. It was formally
the home of the Hon. Ernest Guinness, second son of the 1st Earl of
Iveagh. There are about thirty rooms in the mansion, including several
spacious entertainment apartments. The building looks out on to
Grosvenor Place, the porticoed door is on Chapel Street and upper
rooms overlook the lawns at the back of Buckingham Palace.

Irish petitioners approaching the Irish Embassy on Grosvenor Place, *c.* 1960.

THE GUINNESS TRUST

This distinguished charity focused on building housing units in bulk for less fortunate people all across Britain. Founded in London in 1890 by Edward Cecil Guinness, the 1st Earl of Iveagh, great-grandson of the founder of the Guinness Brewery, it functioned in a similar fashion to the Iveagh Trust in Dublin. The generous philanthropist and businessman gave £200,000, or approximately £15 million in today's money, to set up the Guinness Trust. In order to provide adequate housing for poor and elderly people who could not afford decent homes, the trust first built homes in the 1890s in London, offering communal clubrooms with heated baths and bathing attendants. Since then, it has been building residential flats in Hampstead, Walworth, Chelsea, Bethnal Green, Finsbury, Lambeth, Bermonsey, Hammersmith, Kensington and Hackney, although it is now known as The Guinness Partnership.

Some of the existing buildings were severely damaged during the war and, due to the general shortage of materials (among various other difficulties), the trust was unable to repair them until 1950. As soon as the materials were available, it quickly started rebuilding and constructed a large block of small self-contained flats for people living alone. The Guinness Trust is considered as one of the most notable UK-registered charities.

THE MARTIN HOUSE ASSOCIATION

One of the various charity projects specifically created for women was the Martin House Association. It ran a hostel on Lansdowne Road in London for 'fallen Irish women' – prostitutes and women recently released from prison – who were in need of help and rehabilitation. This hostel offered these women the 'opportunity to start with a clean slate and to prevent them from returning to a life of crime.'[155]

Under the guidance of Fr Hilary Carpenter, many eminent people in London, which included Cardinal Griffin, Mary Byrne, the daughter of independent TD (a Teachta Dála, a member of Dáil Éireann, the lower house of the Irish Parliament), long-time Lord Mayor of Dublin Alfred Byrne, social welfare workers, probation officers and doctors, were involved with the hostel scheme. The members of the association were instrumental for raising money. Dr T.P. O'Sullivan, who visited Catholic prisoners in Wandsworth prison for many years, called for urgent help for more Catholic people to visit prisoners as 'human sympathy is invaluable'[156] upon release back into the real world.

THE GREEN CIRCLE IRISH DRAMA GROUP

This was a popular group in the 1950s for Irish people in London to get together and see plays by their own dramatists in theatres. Weekly meetings were held and the group was active throughout the decade.

THE WELFARE ADVICE SERVICE

With the help of the London Irish Centre in Camden and the Irish Ambassador Dr Frederick Henry Boland, a welfare advice service was set up. The initiative aimed to assist immigrants suffering from hardship. Launched at a reception in Camden Town, Pat Hegarty organised the creation of welfare funds and £120, a considerable sum at that time, was raised.[157]

THE WOOLWICH IRISH WELCOME SOCIETY

The society was founded for Irish immigrants who lived in Woolwich, south-east London and held social events and dinner parties. One of the events was held at the Shakespeare Hotel in Woolwich and was attended by local clergy and members from the Anti-Partition League. With Revd Joseph O'Flanagan from County Galway in the chair, the society often borrowed a room from the local Catholic club in order to conduct their activities, such as helping the Irish in the area.

SPORTING GROUPS

THE LONDON IRISH AMATEUR RUGBY FOOTBALL CLUB

A group of Irishmen came together and formed their own club, the London Irish Rugby Football Club, in 1898. The founding members were Irish politicians, lawyers and businessmen with a passion for rugby, regardless of creed or politics.

By the 1950s, the club had established deep roots in London. It had six teams and was in the process of setting up a schoolboys' section. In 1951, it became the first club in Britain to host a touring Italian team at Blackheath in south-east London. The thriving club hosted many more throughout the decade. Many high-profile people were often involved with the club, which ensured that club events were organised with style. Their annual dance and other functions were always held at the swanky Hyde Park Hotel. Sometimes nearly 1,000 attended their event.

THE GAELIC ATHLETIC ASSOCIATION

The Gaelic Athletic Association, or GAA, was established by Michael Cusack in Ireland in 1884 in order to promote a revival of traditional Irish sports such as Gaelic football, hurling and later camogie (hurling played by women), stating its mission as 'the preservation and cultivation of national pastime'. Along with Charles Stewart Parnell and Michael Davitt, Archbishop Thomas Croke was invited to become a patron of the new association. Archbishop Croke underlined the purpose:

> We are daily importing from England, not only her manufactured goods, but together with her fashions, her accents, her vicious literature,

The Gaelic Athletics Association marching down Whitehall as part of the St Patrick's Day Parade, 1962. A Sinn Féin group marches behind them and the Cenotaph can be seen in the distance. The march through Whitehall on St Patrick's Day was an annual event during the 1950s and 1960s until the outbreak of hostilities in Norther Ireland caused them to give up.

A team photograph taken just before a hurling match in Mitcham, *c*. 1960. All-Ireland matches were held annually at a stadium in Mitcham. The majority of All-Ireland teams had players who lived in London.

her music, her dances and her manifold mannerisms, her games also and her pastimes, to the utter discredit of our own grand national sports ... as though we were ashamed of them.[158]

Although the GAA was a sporting organisation, and not exactly established as a politically motivated organisation, around half of the members elected to the national executive in 1885 were Fenians, and almost all players and members were Irish Republican Brotherhood members or politically active people.

The GAA soon gained widespread support and grew to be extremely anti-English. For a start, it banned members who played or watched foreign games, as well as the members of the Royal Irish Constabulary and the army. Michael Cusack even called rugby and football 'a denationalising plague'.

LONDON GAA

The London GAA was established in 1895 and, along with the Gaelic League, Irish National Club and Cumann na nGaedheal, occupied offices on Chancery Lane, in the centre of London. At its inception, the GAA had nine clubs in London, and GAA players regularly played in north London, at Muswell Hill and Lea Bridge. Liam McCarthy (1853-1928) and Sam Maguire (1879-1927) were key founders of the London GAA.

Liam McCarthy was born in Southwark, in 1853, to parents from Counties Cork and Limerick. A fluent Gaelic speaker, McCarthy grew up playing hurling on Clapham Common. He worked as a blacksmith's hammer man and, later, a railroad man. In 1895, he became the treasurer of the first London GAA County Board. As a huge hurling fan, he was involved in arranging for the Munster and Leinster Hurling teams to come to London in 1896. In 1898, he was appointed as President of the County Board, and continued to raise the GAA's profile by setting up regular championship matches for London hurling clubs. McCarthy commissioned a trophy based on an ancient Irish drinking cup, and this was offered to the GAA in Croke Park, starting a tradition: since 1921, the Liam McCarthy Cup has been awarded to the winners of the All-Ireland Senior Hurling Championship.

Irish republican and avid Gaelic footballer Sam Maguire started his GAA career in London. Maguire was born in Mallabraga, County Cork, into a well-respected Church of Ireland family. He moved to London with his brothers in 1899 to work for the Post Office, which was dominated by Irish workers. He played for the Hibernian Gaelic Football Club and later became the captain who led his team to four consecutive London Championships between 1901 and 1904. With his great leadership qualities, Maguire also led the Senior London County panel to the All-Ireland finals from 1900 to 1903, and he was rewarded for all his hard work by being elected chairman of the London GAA County Board in 1907. He was also an active member of the Gaelic League in London and the Irish Republican Brotherhood. Most famously, Maguire recruited his workmate Michael Collins into the republican movement in 1909. The future revolutionary leader joined to play games with him and became a member of the GAA London County Board. The Sam Maguire Cup was named in his honour and has been awarded to the winners of the All-Ireland Senior Football Championship since 1928.

Around fifty years later, the London GAA was firmly established. London was a great place to play in and watch competitive GAA matches, with a steady supply of qualified players constantly crossing the Irish Sea.

Former secretary of the London GAA, Pat Griffin, estimated that there were twenty-five GAA clubs in the mid-1950s and, towards the end of the 1950s, there were around eighty clubs, with approximately 1,500 members actively playing. Each club had average of 100 supporters. With an increase in number of newcomers from Ireland, many clubs were quickly set up.

Camogie was actively played in the 1930s but declined after the war, probably due to the lack of leadership. However, according to an Irish newspaper article published in September 1950, the London camogie team won against the Warwickshire team and went on to play in the All-Ireland camogie final at New Eltham. During this decade, a few so-called 'newly formed' camogie teams were sporadically mentioned in newspapers. But it seemed like they were one-off teams or matches as no follow-up articles could be found. Alternatively, it could be simply that women's teams didn't get the same publicity as men's.

In the early 1950s, big matches were always held at Mitcham Stadium, until it was closed in 1956. The London GAA was using the stadium in Mitcham, south London, as early as 1939 as the *Catholic Herald* on 2 June 1939 published an extensive report the 'outstanding success of the big annual event of GAA on Whit Monday'. The Tipperary Cup was played at the Ford Motor Company Sports ground in Dagenham. Smaller-scale grounds, such as Blackheath, Hackney, Watford, Eltham, Kimmage Grove and Manor Park athletic ground were also used for GAA games. In 1958, the old Wembley Stadium hosted the first GAA game and subsequently followed it with many Gaelic football and hurling games. The late 1950s saw the biggest crowd, with about 40,000 people gathered at Wembley Stadium.

The 1950s saw the height of the GAA in London. GAA clubs also organised dance and tea events to raise funds for their clubs and games. As an organisation, the London GAA was an entirely separate entity from Dublin-based Croke Park, which had no involvement in the former's activities. For this reason, the London GAA had to be independent and all the money was raised and spent in London. The GAA London kept no official records, while Croke Park was known to be notoriously secretive.

Although the Catholic Church had no direct connection to the GAA, events were often held in parish centres. For example, St Mary's church in Kilburn hosted various GAA-related events on a regular basis.

The GAA was closely associated with the nationalist movement and news of matches was typically reported in nationalist newspapers such as the *Irish Exile*.

As there was no shortage of clubs, they would constantly play each other and the winner would then go on to play teams from other English cities such as Liverpool and Manchester, where there were also plenty of established clubs. The winner would then play in the All-Ireland Cup for the championship.

The Bishop of Menevia travelled especially from Wales to start the big hurling match between Dublin and Tipperary, presided over by the High Commissioner for Ireland in London, Mr Dulanty. The London Catholic Film Society filmed the match and announced that 'the picture will subsequently be released as a talkie and will be shown in several parts of England and Ireland.'[159]

Mitcham Stadium on Sandy Lane was originally created as a greyhound stadium, but failed to obtain the necessary licenses. From the 1930s to the late 1950s, the stadium was mainly used for GAA, local rugby and football matches as well as exhibitions and displays. Every Whit Monday, there was a GAA match at Mitcham Stadium, although this practice died out after 1956.

Maureen Fitzgerald from Tralee, County Kerry, remembers making the trip from Enfield to visit Mitcham with her father, who was working for the British Air Force and consequently moved the whole family to England. (Many Irish people who joined the British Army were living in north London in those days.) Going to see a GAA match in Mitcham was a family event, and likened to attending a festival. Before the match, there was always music and traditional marches to keep the audience – and small children in particular – entertained and happy.[160]

An immigrant recalled his intense excitement upon arriving at the stadium:

> As I went into the park, I thought for a moment that I was back in Ireland. There were so many of our people there. There were people from every county in Ireland, I'd say … I met so many of my old friends and old army comrades that my head was almost spinning.[161]

Although Mitcham Stadium was the principal place for watching major matches, at the late 1950s, this rather old and outdated stadium was demolished and the site was redeveloped as Ormerod Gardens housing estate. Eventually, Fr Tom McNamara secured Wembley Stadium for the GAA game. The first games – the All-Ireland championship matches – took place on the Whit weekend of 1958, and a crowd of more than 30,000 gathered to watch Kilkenny take on Clare in the hurling and Galway versus Derry in the football. Apart from regular fixtures, there were typically matches for Easter and Whit Mondays that never failed to draw a massive crowd.

After the match on Sundays, GAA players habitually went to the pub and then onto the dancehall later. Some players decided to start their own GAA club named after their favourite or local dancehalls; hence there are clubs called the Galtymore Club and Garryowen Club.

Here are a few clubs in London that were very popular during the height of GAA in the 1950s.

BROTHERS & SHALLOE PEARSE GAA CLUB

This team began in south London in the early 1920s.

Jack Shalloe, from Mooncoin, County Kilkenny, was one of the founder members. After being trained in the Kilkenny mines, he worked in the mines of South Wales. There, he became active in the GAA before the war. He is known to have played against Michael Collins, P.S. O'Hegarty and Sam Maguire at Wormwood Scrubs, when South Wales played London. After the war, Shalloe moved to London and he became an integral part of the GAA with Brothers Pearse and London until his death in 1963. The club's golden era was between 1954 and 1964, during which time they won the senior hurling championship and the league on several occasions.

THE CÚCHULAINNS GAA CLUB

One of the oldest London GAA clubs, it was created in 1932 as a hurling team. In 1934, the Cúchulainns Gaelic Football team was formed. Both teams won senior hurling, football and league championships during the 1950s.

FATHER MURPHY'S HURLING AND FOOTBALL CLUB

This club was established in 1958 at the Robert Peel public house to create a base for Wexford immigrants in London. The first officers of the club were Thomas Quirke, Frank Sheehan and Larry Kehoe.

GARRYOWEN GAELIC FOOTBALL CLUB

The club was established in west London in 1937 with Mr McAvidie from County Mayo as secretary, but disbanded in 1939 when the Second World War broke out. Some qualified young players returned home, while the other Irishmen joined the British Army.

The club was finally reformed in 1948, named after the Garryowen dancehall in Hammersmith and the team went on to win various championships in the 1950s. Founding members included John Bermingham from County Cork, Vince Golden from County Roscommon, John Byrne from County Donegal and Jim Nicholson from County Sligo. Jim Conway from County Cavan was the first chairman of the club.

The first fixture was played on a pitch in Hounslow. The team first won its first Junior League Championship in 1950 and went on to win again the following year. Capable players continued to join the club and it won its first London Senior Football Championship in 1956, and won again in 1958 and 1959.

GLEN ROVERS HURLING AND FOOTBALL CLUB

Founded in 1953 in Watford, the club name was chosen by lucky dip at the inaugural meeting. The first game was played against Slough, with the next versus Brother Pearce's. The team regularly played in Garston Park until they were forced to leave by a petition from a local man, who complained to the council when a ball was kicked into his garden. They soon found a new ground and played at Watford Fields for two years but were again forced to move. This time, the petition was made by the Lord's Day Observance Society in protest against the team playing on the Sabbath. After this event, Glen Rovers moved to a new place at Oxhey Park. In 1955, the team won the London Championship Intermediate Hurling Final.

THE KINGDOM KERRY GAELS GAELIC FOOTBALL CLUB

Michael Walsh, Josie O'Connell, Bill Cremins, Sean and Brendan Kerrisk and Jerome Spillane started this club in 1959 in Finchley, North London.

NAOMH MHUIRE FOOTBALL CLUB

This was one of the strongest and most popular teams during the post-war decade. One of the founder members, Jerry Daly from County Kerry, was an inspirational figure and developed the club. John Joe Minehan, also from County Kerry, was a renowned goalkeeper during this period. Another high-profile player was Billy Mills from County Waterford. He first played with Garryowen, before moving to Brothers Pearces. After leaving that club, he became a prominent player with Naomh Mhuire.

PARNELLS GAELIC FOOTBALL CLUB

Established in 1951, the team played their first competitive game in London in the spring of 1952. Parnells originally consisted of hurling and football clubs, but the club decided to concentrate on the 'big ball game' by 1954. The team won their first title, the Junior Championship Final in 1958, and the Intermediate Football Championship in 1959.

ROBERT EMMETT'S GAA

Robert Emmett's hurling club was founded on 20 March 1948 at the old Bow Palais in east London. It took around six months for their founding members to initiate a football club. Its club members played games throughout the post-war years.

THE ROUND TOWERS GAELIC FOOTBALL CLUB

In 1932, Kildare men got together and started St Brigid's Club. Later, the founder members, who were from County Kildare, renamed the club Round Towers, but restricted membership to people from Kildare.

The first meeting was held under a tree in Hyde Park. In the late 1930s, Clapham Common became the meeting place and venue for training, and competitive matches were often played at Sandy Lane in Mitcham. The Round Towers was not just one of the oldest clubs in London GAA; it was one of the few to have survived and become stronger through the war years. Therefore, the team was always able to attract good-quality players.

ST BRENDAN'S GFC LONDON

This team was established in 1956 in the old Botwell Parish Hall in Hayes, Middlesex, by Eugene Callaghan, the O'Regan brothers from Limerick (Con, Jim and Tim) and Michael O'Shea from County Kerry.

ST JOSEPH'S GAA CLUB

'The Joes' began in 1947, in the men's club that was attached to St Joseph's church in Hanwell. The main founding members were originally from County Kerry. The team colours were blue and white. In 1948, the Joes won the London Senior Championship and the captain for the team at that time was Kerryman Tom Crean, who was related to the seaman and Antarctic explorer of the same name. The club was actively playing during the post-war years, was dissolved at the end of the 1950s, and reformed in 1962.

ST SENANS

Established as a football club in 1947, it was a very active team during the whole decade of the 1950s and played against other teams every weekend in and around London.

SEAN TREACY'S HURLING CLUB

Sean Treacy's was set up 1958 in Tooting Bec, South London. The club's first captain was Pakie Hourigan, who played minor with Limerick in 1952 and senior in 1953. After moving to London in 1954, and forming the club with Mick Maunsell, Con McGrath, Paddy Quinlan, Johnny Connolly and Paddy Crowe, he played with Brian Boru GAA Club for four years, winning a senior championship in the late 1950s.

TARA GAELIC FOOTBALL CLUB

Founded in the 1930s, the club is based in Willesden and has traditionally had strong links with County Leitrim.

THOMAS McCURTAINS

Formed in 1923, Thomas McCurtains is one of the oldest GAA clubs in London. It was based in the East End/Essex area of London. Michael Doyle came to London from County Galway in 1956 and played with Thomas McCurtains. He recalled the good old days:

> I trained every evening until it gets dark. There was a match every Sunday and after the match we players all went to the Galtymore or the Buffalo. As a good GAA player, it was always easy to get a job in England. If you are a good player, you will get a job. If you are a really good hurler, you can get a really good job. If you come here – every club is looking for you, at the same time they will offer or find you a job. This is how it worked at the time.[162]

GAELIC CULTURAL GROUPS

The Shakespearean quote, 'absence makes the heart grow fonder', was certainly true for Irish immigrants, as many of whom developed nationalistic feelings and appreciated their culture more once they left home. They became more aware of their roots, joined nationalistic or Irish activities and enjoyed their new-found passion for learning something Irish in Britain. The majority of them became more Irish than they used to be in Ireland, with some developing a republican view. Experiencing prejudice and discrimination made many people more aware of their ethnic and cultural identity. Although in Ireland they may never have considered learning to be Irish, readily available Irish cultural and political activities in Britain helped them to develop their Irish identity fairly easily.

Irish nationalist identity is often linked to perennial icons such as the Catholic Church, the Gaelic language and the GAA, amongst other things. While the GAA was leaning toward a politically motivated organisation, the Gaelic League and the Irish Literary Society were allegedly non-political.

THE GAELIC CLUB

An Cumann Gaedealach, or the Gaelic Club, was established in Belfast in 1906. Due to a strong revival of the Gaelic language, it organised various social and language activities during the 1950s. A London correspondent for the *Irish Independent* reported that the club had an encouraging annual report on its activities for the year 1950. Financially, 1950 was one of the most successful years in the club's history. While the club's social events thrived, its language classes were not so well-attended, however. While Irish people in England showed an avid interest in learning the language, there were simply too many accessible options elsewhere in London that offered language classes.

The Irish language classes included lessons for beginners on Mondays, and intermediate and advanced classes on Thursdays. The courses included lectures on Irish literature as well as lessons in grammar and conversation and readings from Irish text.

An Cumann Gaedealac's social activities were well documented in newspapers. At one ceilidh event which was held in the Holborn Hall in 1951, nearly 300 couples were attended. Another popular event, the all-Irish concert was often covered by the media.

THE GAELIC SOCIETY

Originally founded in 1777, this is one of the oldest Gaelic societies. It is actually a Scottish Gaelic group but it welcomed all people who were interested in the language, traditions and cultural heritage of Celts living in London. The South London Gaelic Society was especially active in the 1950s. Members from Ireland, Wales and the Isle of Man all enjoyed various events and outings such as music and lectures of Gaelic history and art organised by this group.

THE IRISH LITERARY SOCIETY OF LONDON

W.B. Yeats, T.W. Rolleston and Charles Gavan Duffy, among others, founded the Irish Literary Society of London in 1892. It was formed from the already established Southwark Irish Literary Club as a result of meetings in the home of W.B. Yeats in Chiswick, west London.

In order to promote the study of the Irish language, history, literature, folklore, legends of Ireland and other forms of art, the society provided a meeting place for Irish people.

It organised cultural courses that ran all-year round and included a broad range of lectures and readings. Some events were held at the National University of Ireland Club House at Lower Grosvenor Place, near Victoria railway station. The society offered constant outings throughout the year, such as visits to the Watergate Theatre in the West End to see performances of Irish plays. In May 1950, the society's summer session included a visit to Chelsea, conducted by Miss Ridges, a club member from Newry, Northern Ireland and starting from Carlyle's House in Cheyne Row. In June, the society organised visits to the Maritime Museum at Greewich and the Guildhall Museum, as well as taking in a matinee performance at the open-air theatre in Regents Park.

THE LONDON GAELIC LEAGUE

Following years of British oppression, the 1851 census revealed that English had become the language of most people in Ireland. P.J. Keenan, a Donegal Education Board official who supported bilingual instruction, wrote in 1857: 'No matter what the sacrifice to their feelings, they long for the acquisition of the new tongue with all its prizes and social privileges.' As a result, the Irish-speaking population decreased and by 1891, it had fallen to 14.5 per cent with only 38,121 people speaking Irish. English had replaced Irish as the official language of the government, law, economic dominance and formal education.

The Gaelic language revival movement became mainstream, and the Society for the Preservation of the Irish Language was founded in 1876 in Ireland with the help of many intellectuals from an Anglo-Irish Protestant background, such as Douglas Hyde. Hyde eventually founded Conradh na Gaeilge, or the Gaelic League (GL), in Dublin in an attempt to revive the use of the Irish language in 1893. He delivered a famous speech before the National Literary Society in Dublin on 25 November 1892, entitled 'The Necessity for De-Anglicizing Ireland'

and appealed to all people – both Unionists and Nationalists – to 'help
the Irish race to develop in future upon Irish lines'.

By 1908, the GL had 600 branches in Ireland. Hyde insisted
that the GL should remain non-political and non-sectarian, but it
naturally attracted those who were politically active and motivated.
Consequently, the GL members were often involved with the GAA
and other Irish groups, too.

Due to the huge demand for learning Gaelic, plentiful groups in
London, such as The Irish Literary Society of London, were already
offering Gaelic classes even before the GL began to operate in the city.
The GL London was officially established in 1893 and opened its first
London branch.

This cultural revivalism in Ireland had a huge impact on all Irish people
abroad. A contemporary observer noted of the GL of London in 1906:

> In the League, there were dozens of folk ordinarily in revolt against
> the whole trend of life around them. In the League they were at home,
> they were themselves upholding an unpopular standard in a strange
> land, and they seemed necessarily more intense in their faith, more
> zealous in their work, than the folk in Ireland at home would be.[163]

The annual Gaelic service of the Feast of St Patrick at the Church
of Corpus Christi in Maiden Lane began in 1901. The GL set up a
'Religious Celebration Committee', with offices on Fleet Street in
1904 to ensure that it would continue and accelerate in the future.
However, after the local residents complained about the noisy event –
that for many was a chance to meet up with other Irish people – and
the loud sound of uilleann pipes, they were forced to move the event
to St Patrick's church in Soho. By March 1950, it had grown to a
couple of hundred Irish people who gathered at the church.

The GL had its own ceilidh band and Clann na hÉireann band,
and these bands were regular fixtures at GAA matches and other
Irish events. Larry O'Dowd from County Sligo was a regular piper
for those bands. As the regular solo pipe competition champion

A band of female pipers marching past a crowd of spectators during the annual St Patrick's Day march through Whitehall in the 1960s.

in the London *Feis*, he famously played the Irish national anthem on the pipes at Trafalgar Square at the conclusion of the 1916 Commemoration meeting on Easter Sunday 1950. One of the most accomplished and popular pipers in the 1950s, he was highly in demand whenever there were Gaelic sports or other cultural events.

The GL organised countless Irish language classes all across London. One of the most popular classes was held at Cricklewood Technical School, with Tommy Murphy as a tutor. St Joseph's School in Highgate Hill also had regular classes every Thursday evening for children from 7 p.m. to 8 p.m. and for adults from 8 p.m. to 10 p.m. In January 1950, the Forrest Gate GL reported a steady influx of new and old members at the language classes at Upton Cross School. Because this was such a popular and active GL branch, it expanded by opening its Gaelic School on Plashet Road in September 1950. The place became a leading Irish cultural centre and offered not just language classes but literature and history classes, as well as lessons in Irish songs and dances.

Native Gaelic speaker Séamus Ó Cionnfhaola came to London in 1945 from Ring, County Waterford, which is the *Gaeltacht*, an Irish-speaking region. He recalled:

One evening, I was talking to a friend of mine and he said there is
a class of GL in Victoria, on Belgrave Road and I joined the class
in 1947. About 30 men and women, mainly older generation people,
got together every Friday. The class started at 7:30pm and lasted for
an hour. We had a good chit chat the whole evening. The GL hired
a dancehall and organised a ceili on Sunday night on Warren Street.
They organised other events as well like singing. At that time, Irish
language was very popular in London and everybody was enthusiastic
and interested in learning it. I spent with the GL the whole 1950s –
until 1960. I started teaching from 1960.[164]

Just like the GAA, the GL was at its height throughout the post-war
decade. London GL branches were part of all aspects of Gaelic culture
and organised extensive events in order to disseminate their activities.
Typical branches offered Irish dances such as set and ceili dances,
music lessons, and organised social dance events and concerts.

One of the most popular events held by the GL was the London
Feis, or Irish Festival, that celebrates all things Irish. It was comprised
of classes and events such as Irish drama, Irish-themed plays, arts and
crafts shows such as embroidery, knitting, woodwork, cake and bread
making. The London *Feis* was for all – Irish and non-Irish people –
to appreciate and enjoy all aspects of Irish culture.

INDEPENDENT GROUPS

A series of lectures on the history of Ireland were frequently given at
the Corpus Christi Club Hall in Brixton Hill during the post-war
period. Patrick Byrne from Dublin, a notable Irish immigrant in
London, was a particularly popular lecturer. He worked as a bursar at
schools in London and the north of England and later as a freelance
journalist. As a devout Catholic with a great passion for his native
land, he was vigorously involved in teaching Irish history, the Gaelic
League, and the Anti-Partition League.

After the Second World War, the London County Council acknowledged that the Irish were a tremendous part of the city and sponsored Irish events. The council arranged Irish-language classes at its centres and, in 1950, it proposed to add Irish to the list of subjects taught at The City Literary Institute on Drury Lane, in Covent Garden. Due to its location in the city centre, the institute's Gaelic classes were well-attended..

The Anti-Partition League, or APL, was established in 1945 as a political organisation in Northern Ireland with the aim of campaigning for a United Ireland. The APL grew quickly and received support from all across Ireland. Soon, hundreds of APL branches sprang up all over London and other British cities where many Irish people lived. Although the APL ultimately failed to make an impact and was already in decline by the early 1950s in Northern Ireland, the APL London branches did not disappear immediately; instead, it remained in the form of the GL due to the increasing alignment between the Irish nationalist movement and those keen to learn all things Gaelic in Britain.

It is not clear how many APL branches existed in London, what their main activities were, or the details of their members and membership systems, but the section of 'Items from Britain' in *The Irish Press* in the early 1950s printed announcements of the APL branches in London and other British cities on a daily basis. According to newspaper articles, each London borough had at least one APL branch; there were usually two where Irish people were especially concentrated. Active branches were recorded in Lewisham, Kilburn, Streatham, Brixton, Westminster, Finsbury, Norwood, Highgate, Camden Town and Wood Green. For fundraising purposes, the APL branches constantly held dances and other events. Cork man Tadgh Feehan was Secretary of APL England in early 1950s. It was a progressive party in those years.

One of the most notable events that attracted hundreds of Irish expatriates was an Easter Week Commemoration meeting at Trafalgar Square in April 1950. Messages from the Taoiseach, John Costello, Éamon De Valera, Captain P. Cowan and Clann na Poblachta, an Irish republican and social democratic political party that was founded by former Irish Republican Army Chief Seán MacBride, were read in front of a large crowd. De Valera's message emphasised that the average Englishman was unaware of the facts of the case and it was important to bring them to his attention, as no British media reported on the partition. There were other APL events organised in the same year, also in Trafalgar Square; one of the biggest gatherings was in September 1950, which drew a crowd of approximately 6,000 people.

Jim McGuinness wrote in the 'In Britain Today' column in the *Irish Press* on 30 January 1950:

> Decision Reversed … the APL was originally set up as an instrument
> of propaganda with a basis of membership broad enough to allow and
> even encourage people who had little else in common but opposition
> to partition to get together to work for its removal. English people in
> particular were to be encouraged to become members. Many English
> people – Labour, Liberal and Tory supporters – did, in fact, become
> active members of the League. But while an Irish man would be pre-
> pared to rate the ending of the artificial border in Ireland higher than
> any issue in domestic British politics, no Englishman would.[165]

COUNTY ASSOCIATIONS

In America, Irish immigrants knew that they were unlikely to return home, so they promptly set up their own clubs once they were settled. County associations were well established by the mid-nineteenth century, and took the form of social and cultural groups that func-tioned like extended families.

While in London, however, these groups only became officially active in the 1950s, although groups of like-minded people were getting together and helping one another. These groups are unique, as they began out of a sense of necessity and urgency.

As some emigrants did not receive help from anyone upon arriving in London, county associations functioned as a lifeline, because they

Fr Tom McNamara, the chaplain at the Camden Irish Centre, with a group of women in an Irish hostel in Camden.

acted as self-help initiatives. Members of county associations often teamed up with other organisations. For instance, with the Legion of Mary and members regularly went with them to Euston station, where the train from Holyhead terminated, in order to direct clueless youngsters to safe accommodation. Fr Tom McNamara, the chaplain at the Camden Irish Centre, worked hard to find and secure accommodation for newcomers.

Their extended social network eventually helped to build and strengthen local economies in Ireland. Irish migrant workers initially helped their own county people – who had just arrived in Britain – to find accommodation and a job. These well-settled immigrants then provided financial assistance to their county of origin in Ireland by sending money.

People from the same county initially would get together informally, but in order to be more organised and structured, each set up an association. The aim of the county associations were more or less the same – they all provided immediate assistance, such as finding accommodation and work, and eventually provided social, cultural, welfare supports and long-term care as well as burial assistance to their members. Once established, settled immigrants began to help soon-to-be immigrants in their home county who were about to cross the ocean. Some organisations eventually developed a reciprocal relationship with the GAA team of their county back home.

County associations also gave immigrants a sense of belonging and responsibility, by giving people a chance to meet fellow county people, speak in their own language and hear news from home. Many people even met their future spouse through county associations. Compared to myriad other groups, country associations attracted a more diverse audience in terms of social class.

Bridie Shaw, then president of the London Clare Association, noted that: 'the county associations were a social outlet. They gave people a reason to get together. At that time people might have been lucky to get home once a year, or every two years, so here was a deep need to meet their own and help each other out.'[166]

One of the reasons why the county associations were successful and meant so much to Irish people could be explained by their clannish way of life. For instance, the Irish countryman traditionally organised his work, his financial obligations and his social relation-ships around a network of co-operative extended families. Unlike England, Ireland does not have a great deal of experience of unions and benefit clubs. Major life events such as wakes and weddings were all family-centred rather than community-driven. Irish people always turned to kinsmen in case of accident, illness and financial emergency.

Irish society as a whole has a strong kinship system. Despite the fact that the country is relatively small in size, regional accents, dialects and slang vary considerably depending on the locality. Some Irish people had difficulty associating with Irish people from other coun-ties; for example, a Connemara man wrote that he always preferred staying with his county people – or Connemara men to be precise – not just because they spoke Gaelic, but also because he understood his county people better, as if they were his family members:

God be with the wonderful girls back there in Connemara! It didn't take very long to get to know them at a dance or a hooley; but so far as this gang of Irish [Irish nurses and others who aren't very Gaelic] is concerned, I feel more of a foreigner with them than I do with the foreigners themselves.[167]

Many individual associations were formed in the 1940s, '50s and '60s. Some lasted just a couple of years, while others disappeared entirely or merged with the county GAA club in London. Each association elected its own officers, a committee of about ten. They organised social gatherings and much of the money made from functions was sent home for charitable purposes. Their constitution typically states that they are non-political and non-sectarian. During the 1960s, all thirty-two counties were affiliated.

The Donegal Association was the first county association established in London. Founded in 1947, it organised various social and charitable events, and provided financial aid to those in need.

The Corkmen's Association marching in the St Patrick's Day Parade.
A number of county associations took part in the annual St Patrick's Day march through Whitehall.

The London Tipperary Association and the Cavan Association quickly followed, being established in 1952. These groups remained active by organising events and social activities throughout the decade. As for the Cavan, Kilmore Dioceses provided priests – Fr John Cusack, Fr Pat Flynn, Fr John Phair, Fr Sean Mawn and Fr Pat Carolan – as part of the Irish Chaplaincy Scheme. With the help of Fr Paddy Sheridan, the association raised funds for charity purposes to be used both in Cavan and London.

Initially called The Corkmen's Association, The Cork Association of London began at Paddy Whitty's pub, the Lord High Admiral, in Victoria on St Patrick's Day in 1953. Fr Tom McNamara was a founding member.

Around the same time, the Claremen's Association was set up by John Vaughan, Joe Hanratty, Joe McCarthy, and other fellow county people in Cricklewood and Kilburn. The early county associations were easily able to attract high-profile names to their events. Some notable figures who attended were Hugh McCann, Ambassador, Court of St James (1958-1962), who later became secretary of the Department of External Affairs, Ireland; Dr Patrick Hillery, a politician who later became the 6th President of Ireland and a Clareman himself; and senior members of the clergy.

The London Limerick Association, currently called the Limerick Exiles Association of London, was created in 1954. As a non-political and non-sectarian social organisation, it organised regular meetings and events for Limerick people. In the same year, the London Wexford Association was also formed. The first meeting took place in the Red Lion Public House on Kilburn Road in November 1954, when the first committee was elected.

The London Kerry Association formally began in 1955. The Kerrymen's Association, as it was initially known, raised about £20,000 in 1957 in Britain, Ireland and the US to lease a property in Southwark that could serve as a hostel and social centre for Kerry people in London.

As a result of a meeting of Leitrim immigrants in east London, the London Leitrim Association officially began in 1956. The first official meeting was held at St Anne's Roman Catholic church, on Underwood Road in Whitechapel. The first chairman was Michael Mulvanerty. One of the founding members, Jim Fox, was elected chairman later in 1956. Through this association's network, the majority of newcomers from Leitrim were able to find accommodation and work. The association proactively advertised its activities in Leitrim so that would-be migrant workers could get in touch with the members in London regarding accommodation and work on arrival. Members also offered newcomers their support by helping to make contacts and giving advice regarding their new environment. When members became unemployed or ill, or even needed funeral arrangements and travel assistance, the association provided support. From its inception, it has been actively organising various outings, charities and annual dinner dance events.

The Meath Association of London started in 1958, with the aim of keeping in contact with people from County Meath and to assist those who need help. A friendly group of Galway people called The Galway Social Club had premises on Greenland Street, close to the Camden Town tube station in the 1950s, where it often organised dances and other events for fundraising purposes. Eventually, the Galway Association London was officially formed in 1961.

Epilogue

Generally speaking, London has long been considered as an attractive city for Irish people, even though they were coming half against their will. It is estimated that around one-third of all Irish people at one stage have lived in the British capital.

Irish people played a huge role in Britain's post-war recovery; despite this, however, the status of Irish immigrants in Britain was rather complicated. Consequently, some people could not settle very well as they were convinced that they were not staying too long. On top of being relatively young, they lacked commitment, responsibility or a will to stay and succeed. They believed that they would go home with a lot of money, whatever happened. The psychological distance was far further than they could possibly imagine.

Until around the 1990s, finding homeless men with an Irish brogue on the streets of London was not hard at all. They supported the British and Irish economies by enduring appalling working and living conditions and suffering subhuman conditions, but received no help from either the British or Irish post-war governments. It is not surprising that the Irish are the only ethnic minority group to have shortened their lifespan by coming to Britain.

One of the unique aspects of Irish immigrants around the globe is that they retained their national identity, in different ways, depending on the locality in which they settled. Some assimilated fairly quickly into a certain local society, while others struggled at the bottom of the ladder. Many people who moved to London during the post-war years told me that the reason they chose to cross the water was that they could always come back if it did not work out. The decision to leave for America or Australia, however, was not one to be made lightly and required a great deal of determined planning. Often, Irish people who planned to move to far-flung countries typically spent some time working in British cities just prior to their departure as a way to test the water. Then, after moving on to those distant lands, they established themselves and bought a house as soon as they could, because many of them knew they would probably not return home. Although life on foreign soil was – initially at least – equally brutal, they were able to put down roots quicker and formed their brand-new national identity with a sense of purpose and tenacity.

London may not have been the most popular destination for 'the go-getters', but Irish people thrived in the British capital in their own distinctive way. After all, there is nowhere quite like London. It has a certain charm and unique characteristics. The immigrants of the 1950s constantly reminded me that London brings out the Irishness in everybody. There is no doubt about it – all Irish people become more Irish in London. With a steady supply of experts – whatever their field of expertise – constantly crossing the pond, London was the perfect place to learn everything Irish and develop a newfound passion. There was no shortage of eager learners who would motivate you and boost your confidence along the way. Even though it took quite a while to settle into London, many people grew to love the city and what it had to offer.

What's more, Irish people lived between the two worlds and their semi-permanent settlement gave them more flexibility; not just physically, but psychologically as well. Depending on their perspective of experience, London meant a comfortable home, a stepping stone, exile or – in extreme circumstances – a complete disaster. No one shoe fits all. Every emigration story is unique and different. One thing in common, however, is that they followed the pattern of the times and became a part of the valuable fabric of British society. To sum up, by way of Paddy Fahey's words on how Irish stories were interwoven with urban landscapes: 'if you want to learn anything about Ireland, come to London, that's all.'

BIBLIOGRAPHY

Akenson, D.H, *The Irish Diaspora* (Toronto: P.D. Meany Publishers, 1996)

Baines, D., 'The Economics of Migration: Nineteenth-century Britain', *ReFresh*, 27 (1998)

Balarajan, R., 'Ethnicity and Variations in the Nation's Health', *Health Trends*, 27, pp.114–19 (1995)

Barker, T. (ed.) *et al.*, *Population & Society in Britain 1850-1980* (London: Batsford Academic and Educational Ltd, 1982)

Barrett, A., 'Irish Migration: Characteristics, Causes and Consequences', *Institute for the Study of Labor (Germany) discussion paper series*, 97 (1999)

Bartlett, T. (ed.), *Irish Studies: A General Introduction* (Dublin: Gill and Macmillan, 1988)

Beckett, J. *The Anglo-Irish Tradition* (Belfast: Blackstaff Press, 1976)

Bedarida, F., *A Social History of England 1851-1975* (London: Methuen, 1976)

Belchem, J., *The Irish Diaspora: The Complexities of Mass Migration* (Liverpool: University of Liverpool Working Paper, 2005)

Boran, P., *A Short History of Dublin* (Cork: Mercier Press, 2000)

Boyce, D.G., *The Irish Question and British Politics 1868-1996* (London: Macmillan Press Ltd, 1988)

Boyd, A., *The Rise of the Irish Trade Unions* (Dublin: Anvil Books, 1972)

Boylan, T. *et al.*, 'Politics and Society in Post-Independence Ireland' in Bartlett, T. (ed.), *Irish Studies: A General Introduction* (Dublin: Gill and Macmillan, 1988)

Breen, R. (ed.) *et al.*, *Understanding Contemporary Ireland: State, Class and Development in the Republic of Ireland* (London: Gill and Macmillan Ltd, 1990)

Brown, T., *Ireland: A Social and Cultural History 1922-79* (Glasgow: Fontana Paperbacks, 1981)

Brunt, B., *The Republic of Ireland* (London: Paul Chapman Publishing Ltd, 1988)

Burca, M., *The GAA: A History* (Dublin: Gill and Macmillan Ltd, 1980)

Bulmer, M., *Racism* (Oxford: Oxford Readers, 1999)

Cairns, D. *et al.*, *Writing Ireland: Colonialism, Nationalism and Culture* (Manchester:

Manchester University Press, 1988)

Castles, S. (ed.) *et al.*, *The Age of Migration: International Population Movements in the Modern World* (Houndmills: Macmillan, 1993)

Clout, H., *History of London* (London: Times Books, 2004)

Coakley, J. (ed.) *et al.*, *Politics in the Republic of Ireland* (London: PSAI Press, 1992)

Commission on Emigration and Other Population Problems, 1948-54, *Reports* (Dublin: The Stationery Office, 1955)

Connor, T., *The London Irish* (London: London Strategic Policy Unit, 1987)

Coogan, T.P., *Ireland in the Twentieth Century* (London: Arrow Books, 2004)

Coogan, T.P., *Wherever Green is Worn: The Story of the Irish Diaspora* (London: Arrow Books, 2002)

Cowley, U., *The Men who Built Britain* (London: Merlin Publishing, 2001)

Cronin, S., *Irish Nationalism: A History of its Roots and Ideology* (Dublin: Pluto Press, 1980)

Curran, M., *Across the Water: A Guide for Young Irish People going to Britain* (London: Irish Chaplaincy in Britain, 1994)

Curtin, C. *et al.*, 'Emigration and Exile', in Bartlett, T. (ed.), *Irish Studies* (Dublin: Gill and Macmillan Ltd, 1988)

Curtis, L., *Nothing But the Same Old Story: The Roots of Anti-Irish Racism* (London: Information on Ireland, 1984)

Daly, Mary E., *The Slow Failure: Population Decline and Independent Ireland, 1922-1973* (University of Wisconsin Press, 2006)

Davis, G., *The Irish in Britain 1815-1914* (Dublin: Gill and Macmillan Ltd, 1991)

Deane, C., *The Guinness Book of Irish: Fact and Feats* (London: Guinness Publishing Ltd, 1994)

Delaney, E., *Demography, State and Society: Irish Migration to Britain, 1921-1971* (Kingston/Montreal and Liverpool: Liverpool University Press, 2000)

Donoghue, F., *Defining the Nonprofit Sector: Ireland* (Working Papers of the Johns Hopkins Comparative Nonprofit Sector Project, Policy Research Centre at National College of Ireland, 1998)

Dunne, C., *An Unconsidered People: The Irish in London* (Dublin: New Island, 2003)

Ellis, P., *A History of the Irish Working Class* (London: Pluto, 1972)

Engstrom, D., *The Economic Determinants of Ethnic Segregation in Post-War Britain* (Yale University Working Paper, 1997)

Fahey, P., *The Irish in London* (London: A Centerprise Book, 1991)

Fallon, B., *An Age of Innocence: Irish Culture 1930-1960* (Dublin: Gill & Macmillan, 1999)

Fealy, G.M., *A History of Apprenticeship Nurse Training in Ireland* (London: Routledge, 2006)

Ferriter, D., *The Transformation of Ireland 1900-2000* (London: Profile Books, 2004)

Fisk, R., *In Time of War: Ireland, Ulster and the Price of Neutrality 1939-1945* (Dublin: Gill & Macmillan Ltd, 1983)

Foster, R., *Modern Ireland 1600-1972* (London: Penguin Books, 1988)

Foster, R., *Paddy & Mr Punch* (London: Penguin Books, 1993)

Fraser, T.G., *Ireland in Conflict 1922-1998* (London: Routledge, 2000)

Garcia, M., *Ireland's Invasion of the World: The Irish Diaspora in a Nutshell* (Dublin: The History Press, 2015)

Garcia, M., *The Irish in San Francisco after the Gold Rush* (New York: Edwin Mellen Press, 2013)

Garrett, P.M., 'The Abnormal Flight: the Migration and Repatriation of Irish Unmarried Mothers', *Social History*, 25 (3) October, pp.330-43 (2000)

Garvin, T., *Preventing the Future: Why was Ireland so Poor for so Long?* (Dublin: Gill and Macmillan, 2004)

Grant, C. (ed.), *Built to Last? Reflections on British Housing Policy* (London: ROOF magazine, 1992)

Gray, B., *Breaking the Silence: Emigration, Gender and the Making of Irish Cultural Memory* (University of Limerick, Department of Sociology Working Paper Series, 2003)

Handley, J.E., *The Irish in Scotland 1798-1845* (Cork: Cork University Press, 1943)

Harrison, G., *The Scattering: A History of the London Irish Centre 1954-2004* (London: The London Irish Centre, 2004)

Hickman, M., '"Binary Opposites" or "Unique Neighbours"? The Irish in Multi-ethnic Britain', *Political Quarterly* 71:1 (2000)

Hickman, M. *et al.*, *Discrimination and the Irish community in Britain* (London: Commission for Racial Equality, 1997)

Hickman, M., 'Reconstructing Deconstructing Race: British Political Discourses about the Irish in Britain', *Ethnic and Racial Studies*, 1 (2), pp. 288-307 (1988)

Holohan, A. *et al.*, *Working Lives: The Irish in Britain* (Hayes: The Irish Post, 1995)

Hopkins, E., *The Rise and Decline of the English Working Classes 1918-1990: A Social History* (London: Weidenfeld & Nicolson, 1991)

Howarth, K., *Oral History* (Stroud: Sutton Publishing Limited, 1998)

Howe, S., *Ireland and Empire: Colonial Legacies in Irish History and Culture* (Oxford: Oxford University Press, 2000)

Hutton, S. (ed.) *et al.*, *Ireland's histories: Aspects of State, Society and Ideology* (London: Routledge, 1991)

Innes, C.L., *Woman and Nation in Irish Literature and Society, 1880-1935* (Hempstead: Harvester Wheatsheaf, 1993)

Jackson, J.A., *The Irish in Britain* (London: Routledge, 1963)

Jackson, J., *Migration* (Harlow: Longman Group Limited, 1986)

Joppke, C., *Immigration and the Nation-State: The United States, Germany and Great Britain* (Oxford: Oxford University Press, 1999)

Jordanova, L., *History in Practice* (London: Arnold, 2000)

Kelleher, P., *Familism in Irish Capitalism in the 1950s*, The Economic and Social Review 18 (2) pp.75-94 (1987)

Kells, M., *Ethnic Identity Amongst Young Irish Middle-Class Migrants in London* (London: University of North London, 1995)

Kelly, D., *I only came over for a couple of years …* (London: TG4, 2003)

Kenny, K., 'Diaspora and Comparison: The Global Irish as a Case Study', *The Journal of American History*, June, pp.134-62 (2003)

Keogh, D., *Twentieth-Century Ireland: Nation and State* (Dublin: Gill & Macmillan, 1994)

Leavey, G. *et al.*, 'Older Irish Migrants Living in London: Identity, Loss and Return', *Journal of Ethnic and Migration Studies*, 30 (4), pp.764–79 (2004)

Lee, J.J., *Ireland 1912-1985 Politics and Society* (Cambridge, Cambridge University Press, 1989)

Lees, L.H., *Exiles of Erin: Irish Migrations in Victorian London* (Manchester: Manchester University Press, 1979)

Lennon, M. *et al.*, *Across the Water: Irish Women's Lives in Britain* (London: Virago Press, 1988)

Lewis, P., *The Fifties* (London: Book Club Associates, 1978)

Lewis, W.A., 'Economic Development with Unlimited Supplies of Labour', *The Manchester School of Economic and Social Studies*, 22, pp 139-91 (1954)

London Borough of Barking and Dagenham Local Studies Information Sheet No.1 (The Ford Motor Company, Dagenham)

Lynch, A., *The Irish in Exile: Stories of Emigration* (London: Community History Press)

Lynn, M. (ed.), *The British Empire in the 1950s: Retreat or Revival?* (Houndmills: Palgrave Macmillan, 2006)

Lyons, F., *Ireland Since the Famine* (London: Fontana Press, 1971)

MacAmhlaigh, D., *An Irish Navvy: The Diary of an Exile* (Cork: The Collins Press, 1964)

Mac an Ghaill, M., 'The Irish in Britain: The Invisibility of Ethnicity and Anti-Irish Racism, *Journal of Ethnic and Migration Studies*, 26 (1), pp.137-47 (2000)

MacRaild, D., *Irish Migrants in Modern Britain* (London: Palgrave Macmillan, 1999)

MacGill, P., *Children of the Dead End* (Edinburgh: Birlinn Ltd, 1999)

MacGill, P., *The Navvy Poet* (London: Caliban Books, 1984)

Martin, R., *Oral History in Social Work* (California: Sage Publications, 1995)

McDermott, K.M., *The Time of the Corncrake: An Irishman's Memories of His Life in 1940s and 1950s* (Victoria: Trafford Publishing, 2006)

Meenan, J., *The Irish Economy since 1922* (Liverpool: Liverpool University Press, 1970)

Meikle, J., 'Irish and Scots Migrants More Likely to Die Early', in *The Guardian (Society Guardian)*, 25 October 2005

Miller, K., *Emigrants and Exiles: Ireland and the Irish Exodus to North America* (New York: Oxford University Press, 1985)

Mind, *Mental Health of Irish-born People in Britain* (London: Mind, 2001)

Montgomery, J., *The Fifties* (London: George Allen and Unwin Ltd, 1965)

Moya, J., (2005) 'Immigrants and Associations: A Global and Historical Perspective', *Journal of Ethnic and Migration Studies*, 31 (5), pp.833-64

Nagle, J., *Multiculturalism's Double Bind: Creating Inclusivity, Cosmopolitanism, and Difference* (Farnham: Ashgate, 2009)

O'Brien, M. *et al.*, *A Concise History of Ireland* (London: Thames and Hudson, 1972)

O'Connor, K., *The Irish in Britain* (Dublin: Torc Books, 1972)

O'Day, A., 'Revising the Diaspora', in Boyce, G. and O'Day, A. (eds), *The Making of Modern Irish History: Revisionism and the Revisionist Controversy* (London: Routledge, 1996)

O'Day, A. *et al.*, *Irish Historical Documents Since 1800* (Dublin: Gill and Macmillan, 1992)

Mary O'Dowd (ed.) *et al.*, *Chattel, Servant or Citizen: Women's Status in Church, State and Society* (Belfast: The Institute of Irish Studies, 1995)

O'Farrell, P., *Ireland's English Question: Anglo-Irish Relations 1534-1970* (London: B.T. Batsford, 1971)

O'Gráda, C., *A Rocky Road: The Irish Economy since the 1920s* (Manchester: Manchester University Press, 1997)

O'Keeffe, G., 'The Irish in Britain: Injustices of Recognition?' in *Histoire, Politique, Économie, Société*, Autumn, pp. 33-43 (2003)

O'Leary, P., *Immigration and Integration: The Irish in Wales 1798-1922* (Cardiff: University of Wales Press, 2000)

O'Sullivan, P. (ed.), *Irish Women and Irish Migration* (London: Leicester University Press, 1997)

O'Toole, F., *The Irish Times: Book of the Century* (Dublin: Gill & Macmillan, 1999)

Peach, C., 'South Asian and Caribbean Ethnic Minority Housing Choice in Britain', *Urban Studies*, 35 (10), pp.1657-80 (1998)

Porter, R., *London: A Social History* (London: Hamish Hamilton Ltd, 1994)

Power, A., *Hovels to High Rise: State Housing in Europe Since 1850* (London: Routledge, 1993)

Pugh, M., *Britain Since 1789: A Concise History* (Hounsmills: Macmillan Press Ltd, 1999)

Pugh, M., *State and Society: British Political & Social History 1870-1992* (London: Edward Arnold, 1994)

Radcliffe, Z., *London Irish* (London: Black Swan, 2002)

Rattingan, C., *What else could I do?: Single Mothers and Infanticide, Ireland 1900-1950* (Sallins: Irish Academic Press, 2012)

Reed, D., *Ireland: The Key to the British Revolution* (London: Larkin Publications, 1984)

Riordan, D., *Immigrants in the Criminal Courts* (Judicial Studies Institute Journal: Dublin, 2007)

Roberts, G., 'The Challenge of the Irish Volunteers of World War II' in Keogh, D. (ed.) *et al.*, *Ireland and World War II* (Dublin: Mercier Press, 2004)

Roberts, G., 'Ireland's decision to sit out WWII is seen as a mistake on the 60th Anniversary of D-Day' (*The Irish Times*, 24 June 2004)

Rogers, M., 'The London Session', *Rí–Rá*, 23 November 2004, p.23

Rossiter, A., 'Bringing the margins into the Centre: A review of aspects of Irish Women's Emigration' in Hutton, S. (ed.) *et al.*, *Ireland's Histories: Aspects of State, Society and Ideology* (London: Routledge, 1991)

Rouse, P., *Lost Generation* (London: TG4, 2003)

Royle, E., *Modern Britain: A Social History 1750-1985* (London: Edward Arnold, 1987)

Ryan, L., 'In the green fields of Kilburn: reflections on a quantitative study of Irish migrants in north London', *Anthropology Matters Journal*, pp.1-6 (2003)

Ryan, L., 'Irish Emigration to Britain since World War Two' in Kearney, R. (ed.), *Migrations: The Irish at Home and Abroad* (Dublin: Wolfhound Press, 1990)

Ryan, L., 'Leaving Home: Irish Press Debates on Female Employment, Domesticity and Emigration to Britain in the 1930s' in *Women's History Review*,12 (3) pp. 387-406 (2003)

Ryan, L., 'Revisiting Ethnicity, Migration and Economy', *BSA Publications Ltd*, 38 (2) pp. 399-405 (2004)

Ryder, J. *et al.*, *Modern English Society* (London: Methuen, 1970)

Salt, J. *et al.*, *Migration in Post-war Europe* (London: Oxford University Press, 1976)

Short, J.R., *Housing in Britain: The Post-war Experience* (London: Methuen, 1982)

Swift, R., *Irish Migrants in Britain, 1815-1914: Documentary History* (Cork: Cork University Press, 2002)

Swift, R. (ed.) *et al.*, *The Irish in Britain 1815-1939* (London: Rowman & Littlefield Publishers, 1989)

Swift, R. (ed.) *et al.*, *The Irish in the Victorian City* (London: Croom Helm, 1985)

Standing, G., 'Conceptualising Territorial Mobility', *Migration Surveys in Low Income Countries: Guidelines for Survey and Questionnaire Design* (Croom Helm: London, 1984), pp.31-59

Sweeney, P., *The Irish Experience of Economic Lift Off* (Montreal: Bishops University, 2004)

TG4, *Damhsa an Deoraí – 50 years of the Galtymore* (London: TG4, 2002)

Thompson, E.P., *The Making of the English Working Class* (London: Penguin Books, 1963)

Townshend, C., *The British Campaign in Ireland 1919-1921: The Development of Political and Military Policies* (Oxford: Oxford University Press, 1975)

Townshend, C., *Ireland the 20th Century* (London: Arnold, 1999)

Vigne, R. *et al.*, *From Strangers to Citizens: The Integration of Immigrant Communities in Britain, Ireland and Colonial America, 1550-1750* (Sussex: Sussex Academic Press, 2001)

Waddington, H. *et al.*, 'How does Poverty Affect Migration Choice?' in *The Development Research Centre on Migration, Globalisation and Poverty Working Paper*, T3 (2003)

Wallas, A.F.C., *St Clair: A Nineteenth-Century Coal Town's Experience With a Disaster-Prone Industry* (New York: Cornell University Press, 1988)

Walls, P., *Consulting the Irish Community on Inside Outside: Improving Mental Health Services for Black and Ethnic Minorities in England – the Community Response and its Evaluation* (London: The Federation of Irish Societies, 2003)

Walter, B., 'The Irish Community – diversity, disadvantage and discrimination', Paper presented to the Commission on the Future of Multi-Ethnic Britain, 1999)

Walter, B. *et al.*, *A Study of the Existing Sources of Information and Analysis about Irish Emigrants and Irish Communities Abroad* (Cambridge: Anglia Polytechnic University, 2002)

Walter, B., *Outsiders Inside: Whiteness, Place and Irish Women* (London: Routledge, 2000)

Webster, W., *Imagining Home: Gender, Race and National Identity, 1945-64* (London: UCL Press, 1998)

Whelan, K., *The Tree of Liberty, Radicalism, Catholicism and the Construction of Irish Identity 1760-1830* (Cork: Cork University Press, 1996)

White, P. (ed.) *et al.*, *The Geographical Impact of Migration* (London: Longman, 1980)

Whyte, Y.H., *Church and State in Modern Ireland 1923-1970* (Dublin: Gill and Macmillan, 1971)

Williamson, J.G., *Coping with City Growth during the British Industrial Revolution* (Cambridge: Cambridge University Press, 1990)

Worth, J., *Call the Midwife: A True Story of the East End in the 1950s* (London: Merton Books, 2002)

NOTES

1 Dónall Mac Amhlaigh, 'The Middle Nation' *The Irish Times*, October 1970

2 Malone, Aubrey, *The Mammoth Book of Irish Humour*, p.37

3 *The Lost Decade: Ireland in the 1950s*, p.221

4 Kavanagh, P., *The Green Fool*, p.252

5 Jim Duggan interview, July 20

6 *The Irish in Exile: Stories of Emigration*, Hammersmith & Fulham Community History Series No.1, p.22

7 Tony Donovan interview, 10 November 2005

8 MacAmhlaigh, D., *The Diary of an Exile (Dialann Deoraí)*, p.29

9 Harrison, G., *The Scattering: A history of the London Irish Centre 1954-2004*, p.132

10 *Justice for Magdalenes*, p.2

11 Rattingan, C., *What else could I do? Single mothers and infanticide, 1900-1950*

12 Quoted in Dunne, C., *An Unconsidered People: The Irish in London*, p.140

13 The lost people of Arlington House www.movinghere.org.uk/stories/story289/story289.htm?identifier=stories/story289/story289.htm&ProjectNo=6

14 Riordan, D., Judicial Studies Institute Journal, *Immigrants in the Criminal Courts*, p.96

15 MacAmhlaigh, D., *The Diary of an Exile*, p.4

16 Francis Serjeant at Hammersmith Archives interview, 2 November 2005

17 Foster, R., *Paddy and Mr Punch*, p.180

18 Fahey, P., *The Irish in London*, p.19

19 Jim Duggan interview, 16 July 2006

20 MacAmhlaigh, D., *The Diary of an Exile*, p.4

21 MacGill, P., *Children of the Dead End*

22 Ibid.

23 Cowley, U., *The Men who Built Britain*, p.164

24 Ibid.

25 MacGill, P., *Children of the Dead End*, p.115

26 Lennon, M., *Across the Water*, p33

27 'Was Britain Better in the 50s?', *BBC Magazine*, 24 May 2007

28 Ibid.

29 Dunne, C., *An Unconsidered People: The Irish in London*, p.83

30 Harrison, G., *The Scattering*, p.12

31 Tony Donovan interview, 10 November 2005

32 Ibid.

33 *The Irish in Exile: Stories of Emigration*, Hammersmith & Fulham Community History Series No.1, p.22

34 Fahey, P, *The Irish in London*, 1991

35 Dunne, C., *An Unconsidered People: The Irish in London*, p.196

36 Ibid.

37 Tony interview, 10 November 2005

38 Riordan, D., 'Immigrants in the Criminal Courts', *Judicial Studies Institute Journal*, Dublin, vol. 97 (2007)

39 Ibid.

40 Ibid.

41 Dunne, C., *An Unconsidered People: The Irish in London*, p.58

42 Jackson, J., *Migration*, p.66

43 Jackson, J., *The Irish in Britain*, p.15

44 MacAmhlaigh, D., *The Diary of an Exile*, p.14

45 Ryder, J., et al, *Modern English Society*, p.255

46 MacAmlaigh, D., *The Diary of an Exile*, p.14

47 MacAmhlaigh, D., *The Diary of an Exile*, p.116

48 Jim Duggan interview, 16 July 2006

49 Ibid.

50 Dunne, C., *An Unconsidered People: The Irish in London*, p.9

51 MacGill, P., *Children of the Dead End*, p.254

52 Cowley, U., *The Men who Built Britain*, p.134

53 Tony Donovan interview, 10 November 2005

54 Gerry Harrison, *The Scattering*, p.23

55 *Construction News*, 'Irish brains replace navvy brawn', 1 November 2001

56 London Irish Centre, *London Transport Museum: Our Stories*, 2007

57 Thompson, E.P., *The Making of the English Working Class*, p.474

58 Cowley, U., *The Men who Built Britain*, p.148

59 Ibid.

60 MacAmhlaigh, D., *The Diary of an Exile*, p.151

61 Cowley, U., *The Men who Built Britain*, p.192

62 Dunne, C., *An Unconsidered People: The Irish in London*, p.12

63 MacAmhlaigh, D., *The Diary of an Exile*, p.122

64 Ibid.

65 Peter O'Driscoll interview, 7 August 2011

66 Robert Sheehy interview, 14 September 2013

67 www.aisling.org.uk/drupal/?q=node/60

68 Dunne, C., *An Unconsidered People: The Irish in London*, p.11

69 Cowley, U., *The Men who Built Britain*, p.231

70 Dunne, C., *An Unconsidered People: The Irish in London*, p.11

71 Peter O'Driscoll interview, 7 August 2011

72 Dunne, C., *An Unconsidered People: The Irish in London*, p.11

73 MacAmhlaigh, D., *The Diary of an Exile*, p.93

74 Steve Martin interview, 31 October 2012

75 Miller, K., *Emigrants and Exiles: Ireland and the Irish Exodus to North America*, p.263

76 Brendan O'Sloan interview, 11 April 2012

77 MacAmhlaigh, D., *The Diary of an Exile*, p.149

78 John Jones interview on 1 July 2012

79 Peter O'Driscoll interview, 7 August 2011

80 James O'Sullivan interview, 8 April 2013

81 Ibid.

82 MacAmhlaigh, D., *The Diary of an Exile*, p. 46

83 O'Connor, K., *The Irish in Britain*, p.65

84 *Catholic Herald*, October 1951

85 Harrison, G., *The Guardian*, John Murphy obituary, 23 June 2009

86 *Telegraph*, John Murphy obituary, 11 June 2009

87 London Irish Centre, *London Transport Museum: Our Stories*, 2007

88 *Irish Independent*, 4 January 1950,

89 Doris Daly interview, 7 September 2005

90 Dunne, C., *An Unconsidered People: The Irish in London*, p.159

91 *Irish Independent*, 11 May 1951

92 *Irish Independent*, 10 January 1950

93 www.movinghere.org.uk/stories/story239/story239.htm?identifier=stories/story239/story239.htm&ProjectNo=8

94 William Thompson interview, 4 February 2013

95 www.tcd.ie/CISS/mmspain.php

96 *Catholic Herald*, December 1951

97 *Soldier* magazine, May 1951

98 Lee, J.J., *Ireland 1912-1985 Politics and Society*, p.377

99 *Catholic Herald*, December 1951

100 *Irish Independent*, 11 April 1950

101 Jim Duggan interview, 16 July 2006

102 Dunne, C., *An Unconsidered People: The Irish in London*, p.59

103 Jim Duggan interview, 16 July 2006

104 The Central Executive Council of the Anti-Partition League brochure

105 Patrick Kavanagh, *The Green Fool*, p.263

106 Fahey, P., *The Irish in London*, p33

107 Jim Duggan interview, 16 July 2006

108 Holohan, A., *Working Lives*, p.12

109 Ferriter, D., *The Transformation of Ireland 1900-2000*, p.481

110 *Catholic Herald*, 'Catholic immigrants', 9 December 1955

111 Fahey, P., *The Irish in London*, pp.31-3

112 Ibid.

113 Ibid.

114 Dunne, C., *An Unconsidered People: The Irish in London*, p.15

115 *Catholic Herald*, 'Year of help for Irish immigrants', 30 September 1955

116 Ibid.

117 Ibid.

118 *Irish Independent,* 10 April 1950

119 Ibid.

120 Tony Donovan interview, 10 November 2005

121 Ibid.

122 Daly, M.E., *The Slow Failure: Population Decline and Independent Ireland, 1922-1973*, p.290

123 *Catholic Herald*, 'Year of help for Irish immigrants', 30 September 1955

124 Ibid.

125 Ibid.

126 Ibid.

127 Ibid.

128 Ibid.

129 Ibid.

130 Daly, M.E., *The Slow Failure: Population Decline and Independent Ireland, 1922-1973*, p.288

131 Ibid.

132 *Catholic Herald*, 'Irish Cardinal opens London Irish Centre',

30 September 1955

133 MacAmhlaigh, D., *The Diary of an Exile*, p.112

134 Ibid.

135 O'Connor, K., *The Irish in Britain*, p.87

136 Fahey, P., *The Irish in London*, p.35

137 John Jones interview, 11 October 2015

138 MacAmhlaigh, D., *The Diary of an Exile*, p.112

139 Ibid.

140 Dunne, C., *An Unconsidered People: The Irish in London*, p.85

141 Tony Donovan interviewed, 10 November 2005

142 Dunne, C., *An Unconsidered People: The Irish in London*, p.78

143 Ibid.

144 Fahey, P., *The Irish in London*, p.30

145 Belinda interview, 3 April 2005

146 McDermott, K.M., *The Time of the Corncrake: An Irishman's Memories of His Life in 1940s and 1950s*, p.187

147 Fahey, P., *The Irish in London*, p.28-30

148 Scanlon, A., *The Rock 'n' Roll Guide to Camden*

149 *Guardian*, Bill Fuller obituary, 9 September 2008

150 Ibid.

151 Ibid.

152 *Derry Journal*, 'End of an era as the Galtymore closes its doors', 29 May 2008

153 Ibid.

154 O'Connor, K., *The Irish in Britain*, p.84

155 *Catholic Herald*, 'Hostel will give girls fresh start', 20 April 1951

156 Ibid.

157 Harrison, G., *The Scattering*, p.45

158 Lydon, J., *The Making of Ireland*, p.320

159 *Catholic Herald*, 2 June 1939

160 Maureen Fitzgerald interview, 10 January 2000

161 MacAmhlaigh, D., *The Diary of an Exile*, p.27

162 Michael Doyle interview, 3 August 2005

163 Foster, R., *Modern Ireland 1600-1972*, p.370

164 Séamus Ó Cionnfhaola, interview 17 August 2005

165 *Irish Press* on 30 January 1950

166 Ibid.

167 MacAmhlaigh, D., *The Diary of an Exile*, p.8

Also from The History Press

MIKI GARCIA

IRELAND'S
INVASION
OF THE WORLD
THE IRISH DIASPORA IN A NUTSHELL